Disaster Risk Reduction

Disaster Risk Reduction

Teaching Environmental Concerns

Edited by

M. Rajendra Nath Babu
Santhosh Kumar
Buno Liegise
Kumar Raka
Balu I

SHIPRA

₹ 950; US$ 38
ISBN: 978-93-91978-31-0

2023
First Hardback Published in India

Disaster Risk Reduction:
Teaching Environmental Concerns

Published by:
SHIPRA PUBLICATIONS
LG 18-19, Pankaj Central Market
I.P. Ext., Patparganj, Delhi 110092, India
Tel.: +91 11 2223 5152/6152; 96500 28065
E-mail: info@shiprapublication.com
www.shiprapublication.com

Foreword

According to the WMO Atlas of Mortality and Economic Losses from Weather, Climate and Water Extremes (1970–2019), there has been a dramatic increase in the economic losses caused by weather disasters during the past 50 years. Globally, weather and climate-related risks, which potentially cause loss and damage, have increased dramatically over the past few decades. The most recent climate projections indicate a significant increase in the frequency, duration and intensity of extreme weather events as well as severe slow-onset climate-related changes. These pose a growing risk to sustainable development of communities and countries. Many of the impacts of climate change and disaster are experienced through water-related events, namely flooding, intensified storms, drought, the melting of glaciers and salination of coastal freshwater resources due to rise in sea level.

In 2021 flooding led to thousands of casualties in several countries, including Belgium, China, Germany and India. India is one of the world's most disaster-prone countries as it is exposed to many natural hazards including floods, cyclones, droughts, and earthquakes. India started reorganizing its domestic disaster management system after successive major disasters, including the 1999 Super Cyclone in Odisha, Gujarat earthquake in 2001, and Indian Ocean tsunami in 2004. The aftermath of these devastating disasters led India to enact the Disaster Management Act in 2005, adopt the National Policy on DM in 2009, and develop the National Disaster Management Plan in 2016.

The Disaster Management Act of 2005 defines Disaster Management as an integrated process of planning, organizing, coordinating and implementing measures which are necessary for prevention of threat of any disaster, reduction of risk of any disaster or its consequences, readiness to deal with any disaster, promptness in dealing with a disaster, assessing the severity of the effects of any disaster, rescue and relief, rehabilitation and reconstruction.

The National Institute of Disaster Management (NIDM) provides capacity building support to various national and state level agencies in the field of Disaster Management and Disaster Risk Reduction. The NIDM and the Department of Teacher Education, Nagaland University has conducted several programmes in this connection. This volume is comprehensive in its coverage and provides adequate information about *Disaster Risk Reduction: Teaching Environmental Concerns* with eleven chapters.

I convey best wishes to the authors and the editors.

J.K. PATNAIK
Vice-Chancellor
Nagaland University
India

Preface

The Department of Teacher Education, Nagaland University, Kohima Campus, Meriema, Nagaland-797 004 organised an Online Process Orientation Training Programme On "Child Centric Disaster Risk Reduction (CCDRR) from 26-07-21 to 28-07-21, National Level Webinar on Children and Disaster: An Indian Context on 03-09-21 and Three-days' online Training Programme on Engaging Youth Adolescents in Disaster Risk Management and Climate Change Adaptation from May 4 to May 6, 2022 with the collaboration of CCDRR Centre, National Institute of Disaster Management, Ministry of Home Affairs, Government of India, New Delhi. For the process of publishing an edited book under the proposed title *Disaster Risk Reduction: Teaching Environmental Concerns*, invited original articles across the discipline for contribution in the form of chapters from Academicians/ Researchers/ Teachers/ Policy makers / Writers/ Social Workers etc. The Editors express their gratitude to the Nagaland University Administration and CCDRR Centre, National Institute of Disaster Management, Ministry of Home Affairs, Government of India, New Delhi for their support. This book is useful for the UG, P.G. and Research Scholars.

We are thankful to the contributors for their significant and scholarly contributions, and also editorial members Mr. Ranjan Kumar, Ms. Nazia Shaik, and Dr. Maria Josephine Arokia Marie. S, Dr. Girima Nagda, Dr. Anandakumar Natarajan for the review works of the articles. We are thankful to the all the Department of Teacher Education, NU faculty members namely Prof. Gyanendra Nath Tiwari, Dr. Dr. Pradipta Kumar Pattnaik (Head, DTE.), Dr. Sushil Kumar Singh, Dr. Surendra Yadav, Dr. T. Yolila Sangtam, Dr. Rashmi, Dr. Neha Rawat and Dr. Prasenjit Pal for their constant support. It may be noted that the views expressed in this volume are those of the authors and do not reflect the Editors' views.

Dr. M. Rajendra Nath Babu
Prof. Santhosh Kumar
Prof. Buno Liegise
Dr. Kumar Raka
Dr. Balu I
(*Editors*)

Contents

1

Managing the Impact of Disasters
Through Innovative Educational Practices

Anu G. S.

Introduction

Earth is the only one planet in the solar system, where life is existing and lot of species from land and aquatic beings, including human beings are harmoniously living by adapting the various challenges in all parts of this beautiful planet. But the life is not always smooth in this Mother Earth and we have witnessed lot of insurgencies and emergencies many times across the globe through various natural calamities and hazards. Lot of disasters like earthquake, tsunami, fire explosion and even the breakout of the pandemic such as Covid-19, we have been facing and faced in this twenty first century. But many factors are not under the control of human being. For example, if a sudden earthquake/flood/tsunami happens human beings cannot do anything to control such natural phenomena. The 21st century is charactered by the scientific and technological revolution with the invent of artificial intelligence and high-power radar based robotic system. Lot of geostationary satellites are revolving around the earth and updating lot of information from every part of earth every second. Still to a larger extend the natural disasters are unable to predict and thereby we cannot use even sophisticated technologies to control and prevent such hazards. In this context, we have to think about the scope and importance of certain parameters or preventive methods and measures through which we could be able to know and then control the disaster effects. We cannot reduce these effects to completely zero but through awareness, orientation and through education cum training on disaster management we can minimise the effects or impacts of disaster that takes place in our daily walks of life. Hence, the concept of disaster management is all about management of such accidental effects or situations of earth.

All the disasters, which happened and happening across the globe are giving some thought-provoking lessons to the mankind and through that we can introspect and reflect the fact that even though we could not be able to control such phenomena which are occurring anywhere of the globe but when we understand the nature thoroughly, we will get some time-based insights, strategies, methods and measures which will help us to minimise the effects of such disasters and save the life of many. Hence the concept of disaster management is to understand the nature to the best as possible. When the disaster happens in any part of the world, what government and local people are doing to control the ill effects using the indigenous knowledge and local resources all covers under the concept of disaster management.

The concept of disaster management tries to educate and enlighten people, talking about how we need to take precautionary measures to reduce the ill effects of it. Hence, we can conclude that the concept of disaster management is on *the preventive or proactive mode rather than the reactive mode*. Disaster means "a catastrophe, mishap, calamity or grave occurrence in any area, arising from natural or man-made causes, or by accident or negligence which results in substantial loss of life or human suffering or damage to, and destruction of, property, or damage to, or degradation of, environment, and is of such a nature or magnitude as to be beyond the coping capacity of the community of the affected area" (Definition according to Disaster Management Act 2005, Government of India).

Defining the Concept of Disaster Management

According to Sinha (1998) disaster is "a sudden calamitous event bringing great damages, loss and destruction and devastation to life and property. The damage caused by disaster is immeasurable and varies with the geographical location, climate and the type of the earth surface degree of vulnerability. Generally, disaster has the following effects such as it completely disrupts the normal day to day life. It negatively influences the emergency system and normal needs and process like food, shelter, health etc. are affected and deteriorate depending on the intensity and security of the disaster".

An event becomes a disaster "only if and when it results in substantial loss of life or property and a disaster becomes a crisis when the extent of damage done by it is well beyond the capacity of the victim to withstand it and the victim is almost at the breaking point" (Keith, 1996). Bankoff, Frerks & Hilhorst (2003) point out that "emergency is a term closely related to disaster. An emergency might be regarded as a particular type of a disaster, 'emergency' suggests an intense time period and level of urgency. An emergency is bounded by a specific period in which lives and essential property are immediately at risk". Disaster management can be defined as "the organization and management of resources and responsibilities for dealing with all humanitarian aspects of emergencies on particular preparedness, response and recovery in order to lessen the impact of disasters".

The three important terms used in this definition are *preparedness, response* and *recovery*. The first thing is preparedness. When any natural calamities like flood, earthquake or cyclone occurs, how we are prepared to face and handle such situations. Are we aware about the primary and fundamental steps needed to be taken in emergency to save the life of many? Let us explain the operational meaning of these three terms with the latest disaster happened in the form of pandemic Covid-19. Are we able to cope up with the deadly virus which washed away the life of millions of people across the globe? Are we physically and mentally ready to face such situation? Next important term is response. What is the immediate response that we have to deal that situation? In Covid-19, are we ready with some medicine and drugs or even vaccine that can back virus out of the earth? Response is not a onetime answer or one time solution, but it is a solution that can handle the situation effectively. Hence response is that timely action which we kept it led, so that we can handle the situation. The third term is recovery. We all know the pandemic Covid-19 affected across the globe. What about the time to come back with proper medication or vaccinations to all people across the globe? How we recover from the mental stress and depressions-based issues created by the deadly virus? All factors come under the recovery. In short, the concept of disaster management is clearly covered in these three important parameters like preparedness and response and recovery of the disaster. Are we prepared for any such situation? Are you ready for the response of the particular situation? How much time will we take to recover from such situation? If we are able to provide trustworthy and conscientious answers to these questions then we are ready with the disaster management.

Disaster: Classification

The type of disaster includes Natural, Man-made and Hybrid. The natural disasters are happening in the nature itself. This we can't control and when it comes it affects a massive area and lot of people loses their life and living conditions. Earthquakes, Tsunami, cyclone, flood, drought, pandemic, cloud blast, wind chill, sandstorm, landslides, blizzard (snow storm), avalanche etc. are very common among them. The man-made disasters are created by human being without having any vision about imagining the ill effects of their egoistic planning and decisions. In the name of industrialisation and urbanisation and development human beings are doing lot of deforestation and polluting the environment. Lot of agricultural lands are converted into concrete junks and finally buildings are collapsed and affect the personal and social life of the community and individuals. By the usage of illegal pesticides and chemicals soils are polluted and thereby water pollution and affect the life of many aquatic living beings. Most of the constructions in the hilly areas and loosely sand regions create landslide and destruction of assets and life savings. Explosions, ground water contamination, transportation accidents of LPGs, mining accidents, emergence of terroristic activities, deforestation, forest fires, dam failure, biological and chemical weapons etc. are coming under the man-made disaster. The hybrid disaster combines the natural and man-made disaster. The combined effect of heavy rainfall caused by the nature and the deforestation made by mankind combines massive soil erosion leads to massive landslides. Many times, the public agencies and government are giving warning for construction buildings on the river banks and places of high altitude having loosely bind soil, people neglect and do the construction and welcome the hazards. Clearing the forest, soil erosion, industrial waste, excessive production, health hazards all combine the hybrid disaster.

Impact of Disaster in various Spectrum of Life

Social Impact

The social impact of a disaster refers to the tangible and intangible effects on society and the expenses to rebuild the society to the stage that existed before the disaster occurred. The most common social impact on a community involves increased mental health issues, alcohol misuse, domestic violence, chronic disease, short term employment, etc. Recent Covid-19 pandemic affects a lot of effects on the social life of n number of human beings. Due to continuous work from home, isolation from social life, loss of jobs and barriers of gathering in social events along with health hazard of the pandemic lot of psycho-social issues in the form of stress, tension, anxiety and depressions developed in the personal and social life of many individuals.

Economic Impact

Any disaster destroys tangible assets such as buildings and equipment. Disasters have severed short-term economic impacts. The cost of disaster rises exponentially with economic development. Disasters affects the infrastructure of a community in a manner that all other projects regulating funds are stopped and diverted to reconstruction and rehabilitation works. For example, a sudden and strong earthquake creates the collapse of buildings, bridges and power supply and many more in a massive way and lot of funds separated for the overall development of many sectors or domains of the state/country have been diverted to establish the perishable things in the normalcy. So, on many occasions the magnitude of economic impact is more severe than the physical impact.

Political Impact

Disasters fundamentally test a government's preparedness and capacity to deal with a disaster. Government should be aware of natural disaster risks in their region and set regulatory measures in place before the disaster occurs. If a government has done a poor task on disaster management, they may be voted out or political unrest may occur in response to disaster. So, role of government is very supreme in this regard. If a government is not able to understand and control such situations, the government will fail and the political image of the party and in turn the government will fall and create instability about the government in the minds of the pupils.

Environmental Impacts

Disasters have a profound effect on the environment. They cause a temporary or permanent effect on the environment depending on the type of disaster. Earthquakes many times modify the topography of the terrain. Volcanoes release several tons of carbon dioxide and other toxic gases. In addition, they destroy the local land shape and anything that comes into its contacts. Floods cause widespread destruction of local resources and habitat. They also cause loss of life and severe erosion.

Health Impacts

Health impact is one of the most serious impacts of any kind of disaster. Disaster impacts the health of the affected people in several ways. People may suffer from physical injuries that may be temporary or permanent. Affected people may suffer psychologically and face lot of issues in their mental well beings. The health effects may last much longer than the disaster itself. The health effects also linked with social and economic effects of any disaster. During earthquakes, which happened across the globe, lot of people are severely injured, many of them lost their life and those who encountered serious accidents are still surviving with lot of physical and mental challenges.

Psycho-social Impacts

Psycho-social impacts refer to the effects caused by the environment on the social and psychological aspects on individual or community due to the disaster. Several psychiatric disorders may affect the psychological and social aspects of the affected individual's life. The extreme stress, neurosis, psychosis and even prolonged depressions, anxiety disorders are the psycho-social after effects of many disasters.

Also, when we see the differential impacts of any disaster, it is clear that people inhabited in low lying areas, poor house condition of people, severe poverty conditions, lack of information about disaster are the threat on the life of many people. Also, it was found that women, children, widow, destitute and adolescent girls as most vulnerable to various types of health hazards. When we see age-based analysis youngest and oldest people are mostly impacted destructively during any disaster. Location based impacts shows that people living in low land areas, river side and seacoast lines are most prone to be affected by the natural calamities. The people having specially challenged such as visually challenges, hearing impaired, physically and mentally challenged also suffer a lot due to the multiple impact of disaster.

Disaster Risk Reduction (DRR)

Disaster risk reduction is a systematic approach to identifying, assessing and reducing the risk of disaster. It aims to reduce socio-economic vulnerabilities to disaster as well as dealing with the environmental and other hazards that trigger them. The four phases of disaster are mitigation, preparedness, response and recovery.

Mitigation involves steps to reduce vulnerability to disaster impacts, such as injuries and loss of life and property. When tsunami or cyclone comes, evacuation from the costal line is mandatory to reduce the risk of disasters. For this, strengthening of public infrastructure is necessary.

Preparedness focuses on understanding how a disaster might impact the community and how education, outreach and training can build capacity to responds to and recover from a disaster.

Response addresses immediate threats presented by the disaster, including saving lives, meeting humanitarian needs such as food, shelter, clothing, public health and safety, cleanup, damage assessment and start of resource distribution.

Recovery is the fourth phase of disaster and restoration of all aspects of disaster impact on community and the return of the local economy to some sense of normalcy. By this time, the impact region has activated a degree of physical, environmental, economic and social stability.

Integration of Innovative Educational Practices on Disaster Management

India is a country where we can see unity in diversity. Our country has a rich multi-cultural backup and we always try to ensure homogeneity. Each human being is unique with lot of talents. As the above conceptual description about the disaster management reveals that even though in natural disasters, we have no control to minimise its occurrence but in the case of man-made and hybrid disasters we have a prime role for avoiding its occurrence and control the ill effects to maximum. Understanding the natural resources and protection is very significant in this regard. In fact, most of the disasters happen, many people are suffering/ affecting and its impact is so wide as per the above discussed areas. Here is the role of proper awareness and orientation to the community through systematic education and training on the concept of various skills needed to handle such traumatic situation and save the life of many people and minimise the widespread of such issues. Love, affection, compassion and empathy are high levels of human personality traits and these have a significant role in any disaster management. True education is the process of making human beings from ego-centric to socio-centric. Also, educating the heart is supreme along with educating the brain. Here two imports education are proposing to inculcate from the school level to understand the wellbeing of the planet earth and each and every living being. Here proposing the importance of Moral Learning and Moral Intelligence, Socio Emotional Learning and Emotional Intelligence and Life Skill Education-based Curriculum Practices need to be incorporated with the disaster management teaching and training to achieve its highest goals. These practices can use in the Disaster risk reduction schemes.

Moral Learning and Moral Intelligence

Integration of the concept of moral learning and moral educations in schools and higher education is a powerful means to identify the moral issues and guide our students in the proper pathway to respect the individuality and then the community, society and universe. Moral education helps to differentiate between what is universally accepted as right and what is accepted as wrong. Moral education helps to eliminate or minimize the human selfish desire like jealousy, greed, etc. Also inculcating moral values can positively impact one's self, and it can build a healthy positive self-image, self-esteem and self-confidence. The four pillars of moral educations like character and morality, individual and community, civic education and cultural education have very prime role in understanding the duties and responsibilities of each and every individual as a member of this planet earth. The mindset of human beings will be broader through the humanitarian approach and experiential training which we can propagate through the Moral education. Martin Luther King rightly points out that "Education without morals is like a ship without a compass, merely wandering nowhere". Schools are the heart and soul of a child's life. The formative years of a child are the most important. It is at this time that the child's character can be moulded and defined. School teachers and peers are the greatest influence on these impressionable minds. Laying a standard set of values and morals to be taught in school can go a long way in building student character. Moral education in schools is an effective method of inculcating values in children. Practising activities that involve community assistance can give students first-hand experience. Moral intelligence is the capacity to understand right from wrong.

According to Borba (2022), "the seven essential virtues of Moral Intelligence that need to familiarize all students and youth are follows:

1. *Empathy:* Taking note of and identifying with other people's concern;
2. *Conscience*: knowing the right and decent way to act and behave in that way;
3. *Self-control*: Regulating your thoughts and actions in a way that you stop any pressures from within or outside that prompt us to behave in a way that we feel is not right;
4. *Respect*: Treating others in a considerate and courteous manner shows the fact that we value others;
5. *Kindness*: Exhibiting concern about the welfare and feeling of others;

6. *Tolerance*: Respecting the dignity and rights of all people, even the ones whose beliefs and behaviors are we may differ with; and
7. *Fairness:* Opting to be open-minded and to act in a just and fair manner."

Through these seven virtues of Moral Intelligence, we can build moral human beings that are highly committed and sensitive about their responsibilities in the planet earth. Naturally the social respect is coming from the individual respect. Hence the students and youth having high self-respect have respect about others with empathy and they will work for the welfare of others from the heart.

Socio Emotional Learning and Emotional Intelligence

In order to make awareness of the concept of disaster management like themes the knowledge and information dominated education cannot do all. The experienced-based and skill-based education along with cognitive education is the need of the hour. The topic such as socio-emotional learning and emotional intelligence are significant in this context. Give due emphasis on these teaching and training in school and higher education will help them to be sensitive in all domains of their life. The sensation and perception of such individuals are high and they can sense the pain and pleasure of their fellow mates.

According to Fambrough & Hart (2008), "the context of emotional intelligence in disaster management is imperative. Emotional intelligence can play a big role in improving disaster management because the disaster management agencies faced with different needs, wants and characteristic of disaster victim when disaster happens, these may be the source of anger and stress." Also observed that "emotionally intelligent disaster management agencies workers could deliver better service to the victim as they have good ability to handle stress and can understand their and others' emotion better and make correct decisions" (Gabel, Dolan & Cerdin, 2005).

Across the globe particularly developing countries and under-developed countries the major focus is enhancing the cognitive system. But many of students in school and higher educations are coming in their respective institutions with lot of inner conflict and unbalanced emotions. Social and Emotional Learning (SEL) is the "capacity to recognize and manage emotions, solve problems effectively, and establish positive relationships with others, competencies that clearly are essential for all students." Thus, SEL targets a combination of behaviours, cognitions, and emotions. As described by the Collaborative for Academic, Social, and Emotional Learning (CASEL), "SEL is the process of acquiring and effectively applying the knowledge, attitudes, and skills necessary to recognize and manage emotions; developing caring and concern for others; making responsible decisions; establishing positive relationships; and handling challenging situations capably. Similar to the way students learn academic skills, they learn, practice, and apply SEL skills by engaging in positive activities in and out of the classroom" (Elias et al., 1997; Collaborative for Academic, Social, and Emotional Learning [CASEL], 2003). Five key competencies are "taught, practiced, and reinforced through SEL programming are Self-awareness: Identification and recognition of one's own emotions, recognition of strengths in self and others, sense of self-efficacy, and self-confidence; *Social awareness:* Empathy, respect for others, and perspective taking; *Responsible decision making:* Evaluation and reflection, and personal and ethical responsibility; *Self-management:* Impulse control, stress management, persistence, goal setting, and motivation & *Relationship skills*: Cooperation, help seeking and providing, and communication" (CASEL, 2003).

Emotional Intelligence is a very important aspect along with General Intelligence to develop all-round personality of an individual. The emotionally intelligent people are empathetic and have a lot of social skills such as leadership, solidarity, joint responsibility, non discrimination, humanity, impartiality, collaboration, cooperation, team building and a lot of conflict management skills. According to Goleman "Emotional intelligence refers to the capacity of recognizing one's own feelings and those of others, for motivating ourselves and for managing emotions well in ourselves and in our relationships"

Goleman also explained about the term emotional competence is a learned capability that results in outstanding performance at work. Our Emotional

Intelligence determines our potential for learning the practical skills based on the five elements: self-awareness, motivation, self-regulation, empathy, and adeptness in relationships" (Goleman, 1998). Self-awareness, self-regulation and motivation are the personal competencies that determine how we manage ourselves, while empathy and social skill are the attributes of our social competencies that determine our ability to manage with others. Both these categories of emotional competencies of the person determine the level of emotional competence of how we manage ourselves and others. The proper training on socio and emotional learning and emotional intelligence from school level and also the human resource management working in various disasters will widen their social service.

Life Skill Education

Life Skills are the abilities that individuals can develop to live a productive life. Life Skills are psycho-social abilities that enable individuals to translate knowledge, attitudes and values regarding their concerns into well informed and healthy behaviour. World Health Organisation (WHO) defines Life Skills as "the abilities for adaptive and positive behaviour that enable the individuals to deal effectively with the demands and challenges of everyday life". In this definition 'adaptive' means that a person is flexible in approach and is able to adjust in different circumstances and 'positive behaviour' implies that a person is forward looking and even in challenging situations, can find a ray of hope."

Cognitive Life Skills proposed by WHO include Creative Thinking, Critical Thinking, Decision-making and Problem Solving. Psycho-social Life Skills proposed by WHO included Self-awareness, Empathy, Interpersonal Skills and Effective communication skills. Emotional Life Skill proposed by WHO includes coping with stress and managing emotions. The training on all these life skill education by integrating the various methods and strategies of disaster management can help to empower the students on personal and social excellence.

Conclusion

Through the innovative educational practices like moral learning, socio and emotional leaning along with moral and emotional intelligence and life skill education-based experiences, the first-hand training can be given to the students and youth and personnel in disaster and which will help them to open their heart to help the humanity with whole heart during such insurgency situations. The paper highlights the importance of educating the heart along with educating the brain, so that along with the awareness and knowledge of disaster and its management, lot of experiential based lessons, which may be indigenous and local, can effectively implement from the creative and incubated mind of the rescue people to save the life of many during such situations. Even though many disasters are out of human control but through proper awareness, orientation and training using the concept of Moral and Emotional Intelligence and Life Skills, the process of disaster management can achieve its maximum goal.

References

Bankoff, G., Frerks, G. & Hilhorst, D. (2003). *Mapping Vulnerability, Disasters, Development and People.* ISBN: 1-85383-964-7.

Borba, M. (2002). *Building Moral Intelligence*, Jossey-Bass, NJ.

Collaborative for Academic, Social, and Emotional Learning. (2003). Safe and sound: An educational leader's guide to evidence-based social and emotional learning (SEL) programs. Chicago: Author.

DMA, (2005). Disaster Management Act 2005, Government of India, New Delhi.

Elias, M.J., Zins, J.E., Weissberg, R.P., Frey, K.S., Greenberg, M.T., Haynes, N.M., Kessler, R., Schwab-Stone, M.E., & Shriver, T.P. (1997). Promoting social and emotional learning: Guidelines for educators. Alexandria, VA: Association for Supervision and Curriculum Development.

Fambrough, M.J., & Hart, R.K. (2008). Emotions in leadership development: A critique of emotional intelligence. *Advances in Developing Human Resources*, 10(2), 740-758.

Gabel, R.S., Dolan, S.L. & Cerdin, J.L. (2005). Emotional intelligence as predictor of cultural adjustment for success in global assignments. *Career Development International*, 10(5), 375-95.

Keith, S. (1996). *Environment Hazards-Assessing Risk and Reducing Disasters,* Newark Rout Ledge Publications.

NDMA Annual Report (2022), National Disaster Management, Government of India, New Delhi.

Sinha, P.C. (1998). *Encyclopedia of Disaster Management,* Vol-1, New Delhi, Anmol Publications.

Vidhyaashram, (2022). Disaster management Retrieved from https://www.youtube.com/watch?v=v6mPtEmHLD8, dated 24/06/2022

World Health Organisation (1997). Life skills education for children and adolescents in schools: introduction and guidelines to facilitate the development and implementation of life skills programmes. Geneva: WHO accessed at https://apps.who.int/iris/bitstream/handle/10665/63552/ WHO_MNH_PSF_93.7A_Rev.2.pdf;sequence=1., dated 28/06/2022.

2

Climate Change and Spread of Infectious Diseases

With Special Reference to Covid-19

Chhavi Bhalothia and Girima Nagda

Introduction

It has been known throughout history that several zoonotic diseases have turned into pandemics and have caused death and devastation across geographical regions. Many other factors such as trade, education, health care, tourism, and employment are affected due to these highly contagious diseases (Cascio et al. 2011; Epp and Waldner 2012; Smith et al. 2019; Torgerson and Macpherson 2011). The entire world is currently impacted by a unique disease Covid-19 which is zoonotic in origin. Covid-19 was brought to light in December 2019 when scores of people were hospitalised with symptoms like pneumonia caused by unexplained causes in Wuhan, Hubei Province, China (Zhu et al. 2020). "Severe acute respiratory syndrome (SARS) coronavirus 2" (SARS-CoV-2) was marked as the main strain responsible for the zoonotic disease Covid-19 in initial studies (Wu et al. 2020a). Strain responsible for Covid-19 shared genetic similarities with previously identified coronaviruses that are highly pathogenic, including the "severe acute respiratory syndrome coronavirus" and the "Middle East Respiratory Syndrome Coronavirus"

Figure 2.1: Major factors responsible for emergence and spread of zoonotic diseases like Covid-19

that cause stress related to respiratory system in humans (Kong et al. 2020; Zhou et al. 2020). Patients related to market in Wuhan selling sea food, and on site slaughtered wild animals were amongst the first to be diagnosed with Covid-19. Wild animals are identified as hosts of strains related to Covid-19 reports presented evidence that pre-human hosts could be wild animals for SARS-CoV-2, coronaviruses which are evolutionarily related to Covid-19 were found in horseshoe bats and civets which were suspected to act as hosts (CuiJ and Shi 2019). Recent studies have pointed out that pangolins are reservoirs for viruses related to Covid-19 (Xiao et al. 2020).

In tropical areas, higher rate of transmission was observed in airborne SARS-CoV-2 than influenza virus. In temperatures above 30°C reduction in dissemination in the case of influenza virus via air has been described. The effects of pandemic will cause a global cooling of 0.01 ± 0.005°C by 2030 (Forster et al. 2020). The concept of anthropause also supports these calculations, it suggests that the reduced human activity will show us the true effect of our impact on nature, giving insights into how to share earth (Rutz et al. 2020). Due to the short dynamics of global temperature only small changes in global temperature are anticipated. Factors associated with meteorology such as wind speed, temperature and relative humidity can be correlated to Covid-19. Studies from countries like India, Thailand, China and Singapore, established a relationship between these factors and number of cases (Kumar and Kumar 2020; Rutz et al. 2020; Sangkham, Thongtip, and Vongruang 2021). However, negative impact has also been reported. Studies reported from Brazil and Canada revealed that a decrease in Covid-19 cases was observed with an increase in temperature (To et al. 2021; Wu et al. 2020a). In countries like Thailand and Turkey, a positive relationship between variables, such as Relative humidity (%), and Wind Speed (m/s), and the number of Covid-19 cases was reported (Rutz et al. 2020; Şahin 2020). On the other hand, a study reports negative correlation between number of cases and humidity (Wu et al. 2020) and a previous study confirmed this weather impact by providing experimental findings proving that lower relative humidity enhances influenza virus spread (Gardner et al. 2019). The proliferation in subtropical areas (such as Hong Kong) in spring is aided as the Covid-19 virus is stable in low humidity (Chan et al. 2011). Both positive and negative link between Covid-19 and humidity and temperature was reported and a similar association was found with wind speed and Covid-19 (Dantas et al. 2020; Rutz et al. 2020). Some important genetic traits and properties like the ability to bind with ACE2 receptor in humans and shape of spike in proteins indicate that the virus most likely arose from a similar SARS-Cov-2 like coronavirus and was transmitted naturally (Andersen et al. 2020). It was reported that there was a direct relationship between dependency on animals for food and 70 per cent of human diseases by The Food and Agricultural Organization (FAO) in one of its reports (Slingenbergh, 2013). Fragmentation of natural habitats and ecosystems, intensive livestock cultivation, climate change, pollution, and unsustainable and aggressive chemical-based agriculture is another contributing factor for the occurrence and spread of novel diseases that are zoonotic in origin (Allen et al. 2017; Carlson, Dougherty, and Getz 2016; Chaber 2018; Estrada-Peña et al. 2014; Jones et al. 2013; Revich, Tokarevich, and Parkinson 2012; Salkeld, Padgett, and Jones 2013; Schmeller, Courchamp, and Killeen 2020; Smith et al. 2019; Zell, Krumbholz, and Wutzler 2008).

Rise of Pandemics and Environmental Problems

A warning regarding the global rise of zoonotic diseases and possibility of a serious health danger to humans was given in 2016 by the United Nations Environment Programme (UNEP) about four years before the Covid-19 pandemic (UNEP, 2016). It was also said that the majority of new infectious illnesses affecting humans are zoonotic and are associated with significant changes in climate and environment (UNEP, 2016). Climatic changes have increased the spread of zoonotic diseases throughout the world (Sutherst, 2004). This article presents the growing significance of environmental variables, especially human activities, in connection to the origin and spread of new viruses and pandemics.

Role of Climatic Factors

Previous pandemics have also been linked to the environmental factors. In tropical regions enhanced transfer of viruses from their bearer to host which may be animal has been observed, this is due to changes in climatic circumstances (Armon and Cheruti, 2012). Confusing data has been reported with context to Covid-19 on effect of meteorological factors such as relative humidity and temperature on incidences of sickness and spread, data shows dual positive and negative association and in some cases no association at all (Prata, Rodrigues, and Bermejo, 2020; Sobral et al., 2020; Yao et al., 2020). An increase in global mean temperature and an anticipated rise of 3°C by 2050, have resulted in an increase in vector and reservoir species that may exacerbate (spur on) already rising trends of human illnesses as well as cause new human diseases (Caminade et al., 2019). Arthropods usually vectors and many animals have been linked to viruses and are responsible for their spread and distribution (Wang and Crameri, 2014). It is obvious that changes in climatic elements are to blame for increasing human exposure to fatal viruses and for providing opportunities for other animals, particularly arthropods, to function as vectors.

Arctic region was studied to observe climate change and its effects on the spread of serious illness (Kutz et al., 2009; Parkinson et al., 2014; Waits et al., 2018). The findings suggested that as the locations start to warm, enhancement of microbial disease pathogens and vector species will occur. The greater impact of climate change will be faced in polar regions as the temperatures rise the diversity of animal reservoirs and arthropod vectors will increase (Parkinson et al., 2014). Due to direct and indirect change in climate because of influence on humidity, temperature and precipitation patterns, change in non-human reservoirs of diseases is observed. Through the means of trading, migration or tourism the vectors or reservoirs can be transported, establishing infections in new regions where the environment is already suitable for the spread of disease due to climate change. In southern Europe, Dengue was spread by a similar mechanism (Rocklöv and Dubrow, 2020). Climate prediction can aid in anticipating the introduction and spread of harmful viruses and bacteria, as well as their vectors (Harris, Caldwell, and Mordecai, 2019).

Loss of Biodiversity and its Effects

The genesis and spread of zoonotic diseases are intimately linked to the loss of biodiversity (Keesing et al., 2010). The probability of an infectious disease was increased in both animals and plants when instances of decrease in species richness were observed (Morand et al., 2014). Diseases originating in wildlife, particularly, infectious diseases could be identified with the help of previously used prediction models, which showed that increased population density and growth, precipitation, latitude and biodiversity are the factors which indicate the presence of disease outbreaks (Allen et al., 2017). Habitat fragmentation of bats-rich rainforests in Malaysia in 1990's resulted in the Nipah virus outbreak because bats boosted their number and were pushed nearer to pigs in surrounding farms, causing transfer of virus from bats to pigs to people (Epstein et al., 2006). In hantavirus outbreaks, increase in incidence of virus was observed as a decrease in the variety of small mammals' reservoir (rodent) increased, increasing the danger of transmission to humans (Suzán et al., 2009).

Anthropogenic Activities and their Impact

Aside from change in meteorological and environmental circumstances, anthropogenic causes like intense animal production, extensive agricultural practices, urbanisation, globalisation, and contamination have all been linked to the evolution and transfer of zoonotic infections in humans (Slingenbergh et al., 2004). In 2004, for example, increased cattle agriculture on the "Eurasian ruminant street" and production of poultry in Southeast Asia resulted in an increase in very virulent avian influenza (Slingenbergh et al., 2004). Outbreaks of Japanese encephalitis virus (JEV) across Southeast Asia were observed and pig husbandry and large-scale production of irrigated rice was reported to be the anthropogenic cause (Van den Hurk, Ritchie, and Mackenzie, 2009).

Role of Urbanization

Unorganised and irresponsible urban growth patterns have greatly contributed to a slew of new environmental and health problems (Organization, 2010). Census-calibrated model in Australia demonstrated that urban population impacts bimodality, peak duration and prevalence of influenza pandemics (Zachreson et al., 2018). Covid-19 has focused our attention on the ecology of urban areas, particularly slums. It can be said that this epidemic highlighted the global absence of urban planning, particularly in underdeveloped nations. Slum areas in cities and peripheral urban regions are becoming hotspots of Covid-19 in several nations, as well as important locations for SARS-CoV-2 propagation in large cities (Patel, 2020).

Bushmeat Trade and Consumption

Bushmeat trafficking and unusual animal meat consumption contributes significantly to the economies of various countries. Wild animals, birds, and reptiles are traded widely in Western, Southern, and Central areas of Africa, Central and Eastern parts of Europe, and East and Southeast regions of Asia (Bush, Baker, and Macdonald, 2014; Davies, 2002; Scheffers et al., 2019; 't Sas-Rolfes et al., 2019). Hygienic practices are often ignored in the trade of wildlife meat, and people come into close touch with tissues and body fluids of animals. Stores and butcher shops operate as incubators for novel viral or bacterial species that can be transferred to humans (Armon and Cheruti, 2012). According to data, one novel infectious illness in humans occurs every four months, and it is most likely connected to the ingestion of animals that are exotic (Frontiers, 2016).

Conclusion

Integrity of environment has been harmed by anthropogenic activities which have been linked to the creation of new illnesses. Although researchers disagree on the root of SARS-Cov-2, the involvement of human-caused changes in environment and variables of climate in the widespread incidence and transmission of zoonotic illnesses cannot be ruled out. It is critical to maintain ecosystems in order to safeguard humanity from the frequent entrance of diseases or pandemics. Because of the healthy ecosystems and surroundings, this will aid in protection with multiple layers against new zoonotic infections. The urban environment, health, and regulations must be preserved, and policies based on ecology must be devised to avoid the spread of infectious illnesses like Covid-19. Furthermore, more precise worldwide environmental monitoring systems are required to track the introduction of emerging zoonotic infections. To tackle the pandemic condition, the health environment must be greatly upgraded. The Covid-19 pandemic should be viewed as a tip-off to prepare for upcoming difficulties, and we should necessarily focus on factors related to environment that contribute to such pandemics.

References

Allen, Toph, Kris A. Murray, Carlos Zambrana-Torrelio, Stephen S. Morse, Carlo Rondinini, Moreno di Marco, Nathan Breit, Kevin J. Olival, and Peter Daszak. 2017. "Global Hotspots and Correlates of Emerging Zoonotic Diseases." *Nature Communications* 8(1): 1–10.

Andersen, Kristian G., Andrew Rambaut, W. Ian Lipkin, Edward C. Holmes, and Robert F. Garry. 2020. "The Proximal Origin of SARS-CoV-2." *Nature Medicine* 26(4): 450–52.

Armon, Robert, and Uta Cheruti. 2012. *Environmental Aspects of Zoonotic Diseases*. IWA Publishing.

Bush, Emma R., Sandra E. Baker, and David W. Macdonald. 2014. "Global Trade in Exotic Pets 2006–2012." *Conservation Biology* 28(3): 663–76.

Caminade, Cyril, K. Marie McIntyre, and Anne E. Jones. 2019. "Impact of Recent and Future Climate Change on Vector-borne Diseases." *Annals of the New York Academy of Sciences* 1436(1): 157–73.

Carlson, Colin J., Eric R. Dougherty, and Wayne Getz. 2016. "An Ecological Assessment of the Pandemic Threat of Zika Virus." *PLoS Neglected Tropical Diseases* 10(8):e0004968.

Cascio, Antonio, Mile Bosilkovski, Alfonso J. Rodriguez-Morales, and Georgios Pappas. 2011. "The Socio-Ecology of Zoonotic Infections." *Clinical Microbiology and Infection* 17(3): 336–42.

Chaber, Anne-Lise. 2018. "The Era of Human-Induced Diseases." *EcoHealth* 15(1):8–11.

Chan, Kwok-Hung, J.S. Malik Peiris, S.Y. Lam, L.L.M. Poon, K.Y. Yuen, and Wing Hong Seto. 2011. "The Effects of Temperature and Relative Humidity on the Viability of the SARS Coronavirus." *Advances in Virology* 2011.

CuiJ, Li F., and Z.L. Shi. 2019. "Origin and Evolution of Pathogenic Coronaviruses." *Nat Rev Microbiol* 17(3): 181–92.

Dantas, Guilherme, Bruno Siciliano, Bruno Boscaro França, Cleyton M. da Silva, and Graciela Arbilla. 2020. "The Impact of COVID-19 Partial Lockdown on the Air Quality of the City of Rio de Janeiro, Brazil." *Science of the Total Environment* 729: 139085.

Davies, Glyn. 2002. "Bushmeat and International Development." *Conservation Biology* 16(3):587–89.

Epp, Tasha, and Cheryl Waldner. 2012. "Occupational Health Hazards in Veterinary Medicine: Zoonoses and Other Biological Hazards." *The Canadian Veterinary Journal* 53(2):144.

Epstein, Jonathan H., Hume E. Field, Stephen Luby, Juliet R.C. Pulliam, and Peter Daszak. 2006. "Nipah Virus: Impact, Origins, and Causes of Emergence." *Current Infectious Disease Reports* 8(1):59–65.

Estrada-Peña, Agustín, Richard S. Ostfeld, A. Townsend Peterson, Robert Poulin, and José de la Fuente. 2014. "Effects of Environmental Change on Zoonotic Disease Risk: An Ecological Primer." *Trends in Parasitology* 30(4):205–14.

Forster, Piers M., Harriet I. Forster, Mat J. Evans, Matthew J. Gidden, Chris D. Jones, Christoph A. Keller, Robin D. Lamboll, Corinne le Quéré, Joeri Rogelj, and Deborah Rosen. 2020. "Publisher Correction: Current and Future Global Climate Impacts Resulting from COVID-19." *Nature Climate Change* 10(10): 971.

Frontiers, UNEP UNEP. 2016. "Report: Emerging Issues of Environmental Concern. United Nations Environment Programme Nairobi."

Gardner, Emma G., David Kelton, Zvonimir Poljak, Maria van Kerkhove, Sophie von Dobschuetz, and Amy L. Greer. 2019. "A Case-Crossover Analysis of the Impact of Weather on Primary Cases of Middle East Respiratory Syndrome." *BMC Infectious Diseases* 19(1):1–10.

Harris, Mallory, Jamie M. Caldwell, and Erin A. Mordecai. 2019. "Climate Drives Spatial Variation in Zika Epidemics in Latin America." *Proceedings of the Royal Society B* 286(1909):20191578.

Van den Hurk, Andrew F., Scott A. Ritchie, and John S. Mackenzie. 2009. "Ecology and Geographical Expansion of Japanese Encephalitis Virus." *Annual Review of Entomology* 54(1):17–35.

Jones, Bryony A., Delia Grace, Richard Kock, Silvia Alonso, Jonathan Rushton, Mohammed Y. Said, Declan McKeever, Florence Mutua, Jarrah Young, and John McDermott. 2013. "Zoonosis Emergence Linked to Agricultural Intensification and Environmental Change." *Proceedings of the National Academy of Sciences* 110(21): 8399–8404.

Keesing, Felicia, Lisa K. Belden, Peter Daszak, Andrew Dobson, C. Drew Harvell, Robert D. Holt, Peter Hudson, Anna Jolles, Kate E. Jones, and Charles E. Mitchell. 2010. "Impacts of Biodiversity on the Emergence and Transmission of Infectious Diseases." *Nature* 468(7324): 647–52.

Kong, Wen-Hua, Yao Li, Ming-Wei Peng, De-Guang Kong, Xiao-Bing Yang, Leyi Wang, and Man-Qing Liu. 2020. "SARS-CoV-2 Detection in Patients with Influenza-like Illness." *Nature Microbiology* 5(5): 675–78.

Kumar, Gaurav and Ritu Raj Kumar. 2020. "A Correlation Study between Meteorological Parameters and COVID-19 Pandemic in Mumbai, India." *Diabetes & Metabolic Syndrome: Clinical Research & Reviews* 14(6): 1735–42.

Kutz, Susan J., Emily J. Jenkins, Alasdair M. Veitch, Julie Ducrocq, Lydden Polley, Brett Elkin, and Stephane Lair. 2009. "The Arctic as a Model for Anticipating, Preventing, and Mitigating Climate Change Impacts on Host–Parasite Interactions." *Veterinary Parasitology* 163(3): 217–28.

Morand, Serge, Sathaporn Jittapalapong, Yupin Suputtamongkol, Mohd Tajuddin Abdullah, and Tan Boon Huan. 2014. "Infectious Diseases and Their Outbreaks in Asia-Pacific: Biodiversity and Its Regulation Loss Matter." *PloS One* 9(2): e90032.

Organization, World Health. 2010. *Why Urban Health Matters*. World Health Organization.

Parkinson, Alan J., Birgitta Evengard, Jan C. Semenza, Nicholas Ogden, Malene L. Børresen, Jim Berner, Michael Brubaker, Anders Sjöstedt, Magnus Evander, and David M. Hondula. 2014. "Climate Change and Infectious Diseases in the Arctic: Establishment of a Circumpolar Working Group." *International Journal of Circumpolar Health* 73(1): 25163.

Patel, Amit. 2020. "Preventing COVID-19 amid Public Health and Urban Planning Failures in Slums of Indian Cities." *World Medical & Health Policy* 12(3): 266–73.

Prata, David N., Waldecy Rodrigues, and Paulo H. Bermejo. 2020. "Temperature Significantly Changes COVID-19 Transmission in (Sub) Tropical Cities of Brazil." *Science of the Total Environment* 729: 138862.

Revich, Boris, Nikolai Tokarevich, and Alan J. Parkinson. 2012. "Climate Change and Zoonotic Infections in the Russian Arctic." *International Journal of Circumpolar Health* 71(1): 18792.

Rocklöv, Joacim, and Robert Dubrow. 2020. "Climate Change: An Enduring Challenge for Vector-Borne Disease Prevention and Control." *Nature Immunology* 21(5): 479–83.

Rutz, Christian, Matthias-Claudio Loretto, Amanda E. Bates, Sarah C. Davidson, Carlos M. Duarte, Walter Jetz, Mark Johnson, Akiko Kato, Roland Kays, and Thomas Mueller. 2020. "COVID-19 Lockdown Allows Researchers to Quantify the Effects of Human Activity on Wildlife." *Nature Ecology & Evolution* 4(9):1156–59.

Şahin, Mehmet. 2020. "Impact of Weather on COVID-19 Pandemic in Turkey." *Science of the Total Environment* 728: 138810.

Salkeld, Daniel J., Kerry A. Padgett, and James Holland Jones. 2013. "A Meta analysis Suggesting That the Relationship between Biodiversity and Risk of Zoonotic Pathogen Transmission Is Idiosyncratic." *Ecology Letters* 16(5): 679–86.

Sangkham, Sarawut, Sakesun Thongtip, and Patipat Vongruang. 2021. "Influence of Air Pollution and Meteorological Factors on the Spread of COVID-19 in the Bangkok Metropolitan Region and Air Quality during the Outbreak." *Environmental Research* 197:111104.

Scheffers, Brett R., Brunno F. Oliveira, Ieuan Lamb, and David P. Edwards. 2019. "Global Wildlife Trade across the Tree of Life." *Science* 366(6461):71–76.

Schmeller, Dirk S., Franck Courchamp, and Gerry Killeen. 2020. "Biodiversity Loss, Emerging Pathogens and Human Health Risks." *Biodiversity and Conservation* 29(11):3095–3102.

Slingenbergh, J. 2013. *World Livestock 2013: Changing Disease Landscapes.* Food and Agriculture Organization of the United Nations (FAO).

Slingenbergh, Jan, Marius Gilbert, K. de Balogh, and William Wint. 2004. "Ecological Sources of Zoonotic Diseases." *Revue Scientifique et Technique-Office International Des Épizooties* 23(2):467–84.

Smith, Kristine M., Catherine C. Machalaba, Richard Seifman, Yasha Feferholtz, and William B. Karesh. 2019. "Infectious Disease and Economics: The Case for Considering Multi-Sectoral Impacts." *One Health* 7:100080.

Sobral, Marcos Felipe Falcão, Gisleia Benini Duarte, Ana Iza Gomes da Penha Sobral, Marcelo Luiz Monteiro Marinho, and André de Souza Melo. 2020. "Association between Climate Variables and Global Transmission oF SARS-CoV-2." *Science of the Total Environment* 729:138997.

Sutherst, Robert W. 2004. "Global Change and Human Vulnerability to Vector-Borne Diseases." *Clinical Microbiology Reviews* 17(1):136–73.

Suzán, Gerardo, Erika Marcé, J. Tomasz Giermakowski, James N. Mills, Gerardo Ceballos, Richard S. Ostfeld, Blas Armién, Juan M. Pascale, and Terry L. Yates. 2009. "Experimental Evidence for Reduced Rodent Diversity Causing Increased Hantavirus Prevalence." *PloS One* 4(5):e5461.

't Sas-Rolfes, Michael, Daniel W.S. Challender, Amy Hinsley, Diogo Veríssimo, and E.J. Milner-Gulland. 2019. "Illegal Wildlife Trade: Scale, Processes, and Governance." *Annual Review of Environment and Resources* 44:201–28.

To, Teresa, Kimball Zhang, Bryan Maguire, Emilie Terebessy, Ivy Fong, Supriya Parikh, and Jingqin Zhu. 2021. "Correlation of Ambient Temperature and COVID-19 Incidence in Canada." *Science of the Total Environment* 750:141484.

Torgerson, Paul R., and Calum N.L. Macpherson. 2011. "The Socioeconomic Burden of Parasitic Zoonoses: Global Trends." *Veterinary Parasitology* 182(1):79–95.

UNEP, A. and Interpol Rapid Response Assessment. 2016. *The Rise of Environmental Crime*. UNEP Nairobi.

Waits, Audrey, Anastasia Emelyanova, Antti Oksanen, Khaled Abass, and Arja Rautio. 2018. "Human Infectious Diseases and the Changing Climate in the Arctic." *Environment International* 121:703–13.

Wang, L.F., and G. Crameri. 2014. "Emerging Zoonotic Viral Diseases." *Rev Sci Tech* 33(2): 569–81.

Wu, Yu, Wenzhan Jing, Jue Liu, Qiuyue Ma, Jie Yuan, Yaping Wang, Min Du, and Min Liu. 2020a. "Effects of Temperature and Humidity on the Daily New Cases and New Deaths of COVID-19 in 166 Countries." *Science of the Total Environment* 729:139051.

Wu, Yu, Wenzhan Jing, Jue Liu, Qiuyue Ma, Jie Yuan, Yaping Wang, Min Du, and Min Liu. 2020b. "Effects of Temperature and Humidity on the Daily New Cases and New Deaths of COVID-19 in 166 Countries." *Science of the Total Environment* 729:139051.

Xiao, Kangpeng, Junqiong Zhai, Yaoyu Feng, Niu Zhou, Xu Zhang, Jie-Jian Zou, Na Li, Yaqiong Guo, Xiaobing Li, and Xuejuan Shen. 2020. "Isolation of SARS-CoV-2-Related Coronavirus from Malayan Pangolins." *Nature* 583(7815): 286–89.

Yao, Ye, Jinhua Pan, Zhixi Liu, Xia Meng, Weidong Wang, Haidong Kan, and Weibing Wang. 2020. "No Association of COVID-19 Transmission with Temperature or UV Radiation in Chinese Cities." *European Respiratory Journal* 55(5).

Zachreson, Cameron, Kristopher M. Fair, Oliver M. Cliff, Nathan Harding, Mahendra Piraveenan, and Mikhail Prokopenko. 2018. "Urbanization Affects Peak Timing, Prevalence, and Bimodality of Influenza Pandemics in Australia: Results of a Census-Calibrated Model." *Science Advances* 4(12): eaau5294.

Zell, Roland, Andi Krumbholz, and Peter Wutzler. 2008. "Impact of Global Warming on Viral Diseases: What Is the Evidence?" *Current Opinion in Biotechnology* 19(6): 652–60.

Zhou, Peng, Xing-Lou Yang, Xian-Guang Wang, Ben Hu, Lei Zhang, Wei Zhang, Hao-Rui Si, Yan Zhu, Bei Li, and Chao-Lin Huang. 2020. "A Pneumonia Outbreak Associated with a New Coronavirus of Probable Bat Origin." *Nature* 579(7798): 270–73.

Zhu, Na, Dingyu Zhang, Wenling Wang, Xingwang Li, Bo Yang, Jingdong Song, Xiang Zhao, Baoying Huang, Weifeng Shi, and Roujian Lu. 2020. "China Novel Coronavirus Investigating and Research Team. A Novel Coronavirus from Patients with Pneumonia in China, 2019." *N Engl J Med* 382(8): 727–33.

3

Climate Change and Urban Life

Yannam Venkata Mallikarjuna Reddy and
Shivdasini Singh Amin

Introduction

The United Nations Framework Convention on Climate Change (UNFCCC) and the United Nations Inter-governmental Panel on Climate Change (IPCC) mention that the last decade is the warmest decade since last 150 years and 2010 has been the warmest year on record. If global warming from burning fossil fuels is not controlled, the warmness will further increase in the coming one decade.

Urbanisation is the process, where urban areas and cities grow, and more rural people come to live in the towns and cities. Shortage of infrastructure and housing, flooding during rains, air and water pollution are some problems created by urbanisation. Urbanisation changes regional environments and also consumes major part of the produced energy.

Green House Gases

Various activities in the world causes the Climate Change leading to the rise in temperatures and changes in the natural environment. Green House Gases (GHG) like carbon dioxide and methane, around the earth's environment acts like a cover to trap the energy and create warmness, called as greenhouse effect which is essential to sustain life on earth. We human beings and other living organisms, have adapted to the earth's stable climate. Since the ice age, we are having livable environment on earth because of natural environment and its capacity to absorb the minor changes in the GHG.

If more GHG are added to this cover, the temperatures will keep raising, effecting more to human health and other ecosystems. If the earth's atmosphere gets warmed up, it will affect our water availability, production in agriculture. Global warming is being discussed a lot in the last few years as the pollution effects are being seen all over the world. Fossil fuels are being used in vehicles for transport purpose all across the globe, emitting lot of carbon dioxide. Climate change is going to create many issues, like rise in sea levels, lessening of ice surface areas, heat waves across the globe, changes in the weather patterns and thus it effects the earth's ecosystem.

Human Impact

Scientific developments may be considered as one of the main factors of Climate Change and many researchers are working on the cause and effects of the scientific activities across the globe. They are trying to study the increase of carbon dioxide, and the global effects seen across the sectors.

Many studies are also being done on heavy down pour of rains, drought in some areas, effects on agriculture, change in the fish availability and extinction of some species. The decrease in the agriculture production of some food items and its effect on the per capita nutrition diet availability is also being studied by the scientists. The rural and ethnic people may not understand and foresee the fast-approaching changes in the climate by the global warming.

Natural Factors Contributing to Changes in Global Energy Balance

The Earth's climate is dependent on the energy balance that happens, based on the incoming and outgoing radiation energy from the Sun. As discussed, most of the absorption happens on the earth's surface and most of the emission happens in the atmosphere. There will be certain percentage of gap in this absorption and emission process, resulting in the natural climate change effect. These natural factors are being taken care by the natural eco system. The global warming is changing this fine natural cycle balance, because of the release of more greenhouse gases.

Deforestation

Clearing of earth's surface on a large scale from forest cover results in the change of the land usage and indirectly on the land quality, resulting in climate change. Climate and forest linkage is much needed to control the changes in the natural eco system. The deforestation is also affecting the native animals and other living organisms, causing extinction of many species. Also, forests help in maintaining the humidity levels. Lesser the forest area, the more dry environment will form on the land area resulting in droughts, which in turn will result in less rainfall and thus lesser re-generation of the forest cover.

Urbanisation

Urbanisation can be defined in simple terms as the movement of rural population to urban areas, and is a special character of the human civilisation. Urbanisation is the focus centre of social life, economy, and politics. Urbanisation in general seen as having more disadvantages than advantages in the environmental sustainability studies. It is seen as an advantage in terms of employments, production and in development of economy.

By 2050, UN reports predict more urbanisation in almost all countries. Urbanisation is going to become a driving force in the economic development. The present government policies across the globe also encourage the migration to urban areas, for providing cheap labour to the industries.

The importance of Urbanisation Data is being seen by many policy makers. When world population is doubling, at the same time the urban population is tripling, show causing the need of research focus on urbanisation. World Bank and UN provide reliable data on global urbanisation trends.

In the last two centuries, mega cities with more than 10 million population had emerged, and the number of metropolitan cities is increasing. As per the UN reports, the recent 2021 population data trends show the decrease of the urban population in China, the high populated country. As per the analysis the urban low fertility rate is driving less population growth in cities, when compared to rural areas. This will further increase the rural migration to urban areas.

Disadvantages and Effects of Urbanisation

Urbanisation has increased cost of living. Because of more requirement for transport on the same road network, the traffic and road congestion are becoming a common phenomenon in almost all the urban areas around the world creating many environmental effects. The food consumption patterns are changing in the urban areas. The consumption of energy and water is increasing. More land is being converted for housing facilities and other infrastructure. This is resulting in urban pollution, affecting the urban life and health. Energy consumption is more in rural villages. Cities are becoming warmer than rural areas by heat waves. Cloudiness and fog formations are routine. More land usage reduces the infiltration of rainwater and thus lower the water table. Inadequate water and sanitation, solid waste disposal, and industrial pollution are the environmental problems the urban areas are facing now and respiratory infections and other diseases are increasing.

Urbanisation in India

As per the UN reports, India will have the second highest urban population soon. India when compared to other developed countries is generating lesser pollution and affecting the climate change, based on per capita calculations because of its huge population. This is because of the rural areas having relatively lower energy and transportation utilisation.

Rising sea levels will be affecting many coastal cities in India. 5,700 km coastal line of India has many urban areas with high density population. The regions, which are within ten kilometers from the sea shore have about six crore urban population in our country as per the reports of Asian Development Bank (ADB). With a raise of about 30 cm in sea level, 50 per cent of these populations will be affected. Cities with low elevation levels of about two meters are more likely to suffer by flooding during high tides. Problem of salinisation of water sources in these cities may also result in the destruction of ecosystems and natural resources.

Water and Sanitation

Climate changes also create changes in the rainfall over the urban areas and increasing at an alarming rate in the last two decades. Urbanisation is creating water supply shortages in urban areas. The salination and reduction in ground water levels will decrease further the water availability in the urban areas. Also, the rapid increase in the rain fall run off will have effect on the sanitation system by clogging and overflowing.

Heat Waves in India

Cities are becoming warmer than their surrounding areas by two to six degrees. Further this will get worse because of global warming. On 30 April 2022, temperatures in the capital Delhi reached 43.5°C for the third day in a row (NDTV, swachh, 2022). The heat has come unusually early, with the hottest March since records began in 1901. Heat waves are affecting large areas in India, including coastal areas and states at higher elevations which are normally cooler. The number of heat wave days in India, when the maximum temperature is 5°C or more above average, increased from 413 days in the decade of 1990 to 600 days in 2020. The impacts are felt in urban cities, having high density of buildings, asphalt and concrete. The absence of vegetation also creates heat islands.

Effect on Wheat Production in India

India is second in the production of staple food — wheat. During 2021 the highest heat wave was observed in the northern India and a reduction in the wheat crop yields, leading to debate on food security. Wheat crop is dependent on climate conditions especially the temperatures. The final stage of wheat crop requires favourable heat conditions. Indian farmers depend on the regular climate patterns data to sow the wheat crop. But the climate changes happening are making their predictions wrong leading to the production losses.

As per the UN climate data, India is one among the top five countries facing heat waves that may have serious effect on the agriculture production. This is also affecting the rural poor people who are more of small land peasants dependent on their crop output. Because of the heat waves, the UN is projecting up to 25 per cent less yields from the northern India states like Punjab, Haryana, Uttar Pradesh and Madhya Pradesh (NDTV, swachh, 2022).

Effect on Bee Population

Pesticides and other agro-chemicals are killing bees and other pollinators. The reduction in the bees will have a big impact on our future country's food production especially in horticulture crops. (Chronicle, 2022).

Effects on Poor People

Climate change effects in the urban areas had a direct effect on the poor and migrant people, and the people living in slums. They already suffer from lack of basic facilities, and the climate change adds to their daily insecurities. Because of the climate change effect, more floods may be in Ganges and Brahmaputra plains. The coastal areas may face the frequent tides because of sea-level rise. This may add up to the more migration of that rural people to the urban areas, further keeping stress on the infrastructure.

Global Climate Change – Threats to Humankind

Ice melting: As the temperature increases, the climate conditions change very fast all across the world, independent of pollution causing regions. The fresh water reserves in the polar caps are fast melting and adding up to the sea levels rise affecting coastal cities. The rise will be much more in the coming decades if the proper mitigation measures are not taken collectively by all the countries.

Migrations: Climate change will result in the drought in many areas and will affect the rural poor people. Also, the frequency of floods will also cause damages to the crops forcing more rural to urban migration.

Economic impacts: Cities are the driving forces for many countries economy. Less water availability, less food production, changes in the food availability will affect many economies.

Impact of urbanisation and its buildings: UN estimates that half of the urban GHG emissions are contributed by buildings, which uses fossil fuel generated energy for its heating and cooling needs (www.undp.org, 2022). Present building construction uses more cement and glass, rather than the conventional material. This raw materials production creates more GHG. The shift from the normal to luxury living is resulting in the usage of more energy per building area and thus is contributing indirectly to the climate change.

Mitigation Measures

Sustainable living is about our life style and also planning for the better living of others. Almost everyone is dependent on natural environment to meet their basic needs. As the human beings started aspiring more facilities, there is a stress built up on the environment. Sustainable consumption and production should be the part of daily living.

Recycling helps to preserve the environment, reduces waste generation and methane production. It helps in reducing production cost, saving energy thus decreases the fossil fuel usage. With urbanisation increase, governments are making policies for compulsorily recycling, by making the extended producers responsibility rules and also mandating for more shell life designs.

Urban waste management: Major Indian metros such as Municipal Solid Waste (MSW) generation are increasing manifold. And their landfills are functioning way beyond their life span. Swachh Bharat mission 1.0 was launched by Government of India in 2014 and updated Swachh Bharat mission 2.0 in 2021, for creating effective SWM in the country by 2030. About 10.9 crore Individual Household Latrines (IHHLs) have been constructed in the country as of February 2022 (Bureau, 2022). By having toilets in all the households, many towns and villages became open defecation-free places and helped in creating hygienic environments.

Infrastructure development for collection of waste, creation of landfills, compost units was planned.

Redesigning cities: Better city town planning policies with the measures to adopt the systems, which can mitigate the climate change, are being planned (www.undp.org, 2022). The cities infrastructure should be vulnerable resistant to the climate change. The city should have more green spaces to absorb the air pollution, use of energy saving lights like LEDs.

Sustainable Agriculture is a system that can indefinitely sustain itself without degrading the land, environment, people, with a long-term viability. UN encourages sustainable agriculture to mitigate the climate change in rural areas. (www.undp.org, 2022). Sustainable agriculture is most important and contributes in a positive way to society, the environment and the economy.

Smart urban policies: Architects should plan cities designed with interconnected streets, parks, and amenities that will reduce emissions. Policies like transport vehicles using high energy efficient engines are to be encouraged. Speed limits can be incorporated. Electric vehicles can replace the fossil fuel vehicles. Urban forest areas have to be included in the master plantation, which will reduce energy use by lowering ambient air temperatures.

An impact assessment of urbanisation on the environment must be taken up periodically. Energy efficiency and conservation have to be encouraged by the government by giving incentives. Green industrial zones in rural areas, promoting renewable resources and new energy technologies, affordable housing for the poor, drainage infrastructure and climate forecast technologies must be developed. Urban Environmental Policy Challenges have to be incorporated in urban planning as per the UNFCC framework to control the global warming and thus the climate change.

Organisations Working on Urbanisation and Climate Change

United Nations organisations are creating common platforms to discuss the global warming issues. As the effects are going to create tragedy of commons, irrespective of the countries responsible for the climate change, UN agencies roles and functions are at the limelight.

- *UNEP (United Nations Environment Programmes)* focuses on climate sustainability and does many programmes across the globe. It works under the concept of single environment, as the climate change is a universal effect and not of a single country.
- *UN-HABITAT* is a United Nations agency which works on the urbanisation and related sectors. Its main aim is towards the creation of a better urban future, with presence in all the major urban areas of the world. It collects the information of the good practices in the urban areas and the knowledge is being shared with the other areas for the creation of sustainable urban living conditions.
- *UN-IPCC (United Nations Inter-governmental Panel on Climate Change)* works basically on the assessment part of the climate mitigation. It collects and maintains the information based on each country's activities. Every country has promised to achieve the Net carbon based on their internal action plans.
- *UNFCC (United Nations Framework Convention on Climate Change)* was formed to look into the aspects of the climate change mitigation by different countries. UNFCC works to consider the special needs of the developing countries for their sustainable development with the help of international economic system.

Conclusion

The reason for the destruction of forests atmosphere, and other natural ecosystems is because of the over-exploitation by human beings in the last few centuries. The industrialisation has further escalated the damage. We human beings cannot be healthy with a damaged earth and its resources. WHO mentions that the majority of the present people are inhaling polluted air, when compared to the century old situation. The present air is laden with poisonous gases like dioxins and furans to the greenhouse gases. The fine particulate material is increasing in urban areas, causing serious allergies and respiratory diseases. The rapid urbanisation has increased the consumption of fossil fuels for transport and energy needs. The pollution in urban areas is also prevalent in the water and the soil top layer. Because of the no boundaries and the quick spread of this pollution to the nearby areas, the crop production and hence the food chain is getting affected.

This climate change will result in the change in the natural eco-system and will result in spread of diseases and other effects.

Major change in the behaviour and thinking of the people in India has to come to reduce the pollution in the urban areas. Even the government programmes like Swachh Bharat campaign or government policies can be effectively implemented, only with the involvement of the public at large. There is a need to increase the public awareness about the need to keep the natural system for the future generation to survive, and also for the overall environmental and global health. Urbanisation cannot be stopped for various reasons, and its development should take place but not at the cost of nature.

Post covid, the health of a person or family is not only the concern, but of the overall human beings. We have seen the whole world getting locked down because of one virus. Similarly, the climate change effects are going to affect the whole world, irrespective of the persons or regions who are contributing the greenhouse gases. Any disruption in the food chain not only effects the human beings but also other living organisms, resulting some species getting extinct soon.

Urbanisation is happening in the entire world. All the urban areas are facing the climate change effects and are deprived of clean air, clean and safe drinking water and food. Hot wave conditions are affecting the agriculture, making less productivity thus affecting more rural migration to urban areas. This is causing much more stress on the urban infrastructure. The raising coat of living, rural migration increasing the urbanisation, scarcity of resources in urban areas leads to the damage of natural environment, and thus effects the urban life. The health and wellbeing of urban people is dependent on policies and reforms. Then only the ecological sustainability can be achieved in the urban areas. Climate change and global warming awareness among the people has to be taken up on priority.

The urbanisation should be a planned activity based on the patterns of migration and the capability of the local natural environment. Instead of having the existing cities to go, the concept of cluster cities, satellite townships have to be planned. Linear urban cities expansion in terms of land area is observed to cause more pollution and a major cause for the climate change. India is experiencing rapid urbanisation, and in the next decade will maintain accelerating urbanisation and 50 per cent of the people will be living in towns and cities.

Besides having a sustainable urbanisation plan in place, we need to study the migration patterns and the needs of the urban areas to provide them better living conditions. For any urban eco-system there is a limit of capacity to sustain. It is the time that everyone should work on single agenda of reducing the generation of greenhouse gases and thus keep global warming under control. The urbanisation in the world is a need and the same should not be at the cost of having the effects of the climate change. Urban areas should be like a safer sustainable place to live on for all the living organisms.

Climate change also has an effect on the animal and bird species in the urban areas. The urbanisation is reducing the green spaces because of the greed of the human beings using all the spaces for their needs. The small species like squirrels, sparrows and many used to live in urban areas are getting reduced. There is a need to consider these types of species requirement also in the urban living planning by the government. Also because of the pollution and heat waves, many small plant species, and trees of that regions are getting extinct. There is a need to conserve the same for our future generations. All these animals, birds and plants require suitable eco-system, shelter and food to survive, which has to be included for achieving sustainable urbanisation. Urban runoff, that is the rain water stagnation also has effects on the ground water conditions, which in turn is affecting many unseen bacteria and small organisms in the soil strata. These are required for the growth of the plants in the urban areas.

This chapter paper covered broadly the concept of urbanisation, urban lives getting effected by the climate change and the mitigation measures for the sustainable urban areas. There is a further in-depth need to look into the multi aspects of the urban policies, climate change effects, and at large the measures needed for creating sustainable urban living.

References

Asian Development Bank. (n.d.). Retrieved December 15, 2021, from https://www.adb.org/

Central Pollution Control Board. CPCB. (n.d.). Retrieved May 5, 2022, from https://www.cpcb.nic.in/

Environment, U.N. (n.d.). UN environment programme. UNEP. Retrieved June 15, 2022, from https://www.unep.org/

Government notifies guidelines on extended producers' responsibility on plastic packaging under Plastic Waste Management Rules, 2016. Press Information Bureau. (n.d.). Retrieved July 5, 2022, from https://pib.gov.in/PressReleaseIframePage.aspx?PRID= 1797158

Latest News, opinion, analysis on Environment & Science Issues: India, South Asia. *Down To Earth*. (n.d.). Retrieved May 5, 2022, from https://www.downtoearth.org.in/

Pulipaka, B. (2022, May 13). Experts for study on Bee Population. *Deccan Chronicle*. Retrieved May 5, 2022, from http://www.deccanchronicle.com/lifestyle/environment/130522/experts-for-study-on-bee-population.html

The Intergovernmental Panel on Climate Change. IPCC. (n.d.). Retrieved June 15, 2022, from https://www.ipcc.ch/

The official website of Ministry of Environment, forest and climate ... (n.d.). Retrieved June 15, 2022, from https://moef.gov.in/

United Nations Development Programme. UNDP. (n.d.). Retrieved June 15, 2022, from https://www.undp.org/

United Nations Framework for Climate Change. (2022). Unfccc.int. (n.d.). Retrieved May 5, 2022, from https://unfccc.int/

World Energy Resources 2016. World Energy Council. (n.d.). Retrieved May 5, 2022, from https://www.worldenergy.org/publications/entry/world-energy-resources-2016

Written By: Anisha Bhatia |. (2017, April 17). Swachh India: Guide to Solid Waste Management Rules 2016. NDTV. Retrieved May 5, 2022, from https://swachhindia.ndtv.com/swachh-india-guide-solid-waste-management-rules-2016-6253/

4

Role of Disruptive Technology in Disaster Risk Management

Implications for Change in India

Deepika Chauhan and I. Muthuchamy

Introduction

India is the world's next most crowded country, particularly defenseless to natural calamities. It also experiences cyclic weather actions, large monsoon rains, floods, periods of high temperatures, hunger, and other natural disasters are common due to its geographic location. Consequently, the situation is exacerbated by the dense population in high-risk areas from 1674 to 2014. The share of the global population at ages 65 and above is projected to rise from 10 percent in 2022 to 16 percent in 2050.

"Internet of things, machine intelligence, drone tech, prescriptive modeling, risk modeling, and remote monitoring are just a few examples of technological innovations are all gaining traction globally. The field of catastrophe risk is being transformed by technologies such as sensing and others management and reduction" (Monique Kuglitsch, Arif Albayrak et al., 2022). The implementation of these ideas can be possible with the help of advancement of digital technology. However, the availability and distribution of these new technologies vary at different places. This is further divided into developed and developing countries separated into less and more income. It has an impact on the cloud computing accessibility and utility in various disaster management scenarios beginning and after the event zones. Natural disasters have a huge influence on a country's economic and social resources. The total cost of these calamities was USD 163 billion (Williams, R., 2014). The utilisation of information and communication technology for disaster risk management is examined in this paper. The study looked at the review of literature and case studies, as well as the administration survey that gathered input from regional national digital rights management agencies. While they have good access to technical connectivity and a society of sharing information, there are challenges with the agreed framework, as well as the ability and affordability of human resources in information communication technology. For that local digital rights management sector would benefit from implementing an urgent technology human capacity development programme and enhancing information technology governance.

Due to technical advancement accessibility to technology, such as the non-profit sector, is being offered digital solutions. The public health sector, which "must connect substantial numbers of people in remote and risky regions in order to supply crucial materials quickly and efficiently", is one of the most significant societal benefits of technology (Manish Sharma, Nand Kumar). Societies have long struggled to respond to emergencies quickly and effectively with the help of new technologies rescues are finding it easier to identify pressure, share in order, and plan emergency operations. Some of the most modern emergency response technologies are prepared to alter the way people respond to natural calamities by analysing and organising their actions.

Artificial Intelligence (AI)

According to Dale Kunce, co-founder of Missing Maps and CEO of the American Red Cross as someone who has worked on the ground with the Red Cross, having access to accurate data essential in emergency planning and disaster response, "However, there are still enormous portions of the world that have not been mapped for making disaster preparedness and response much. It is still more difficult. That is why we are collaborating

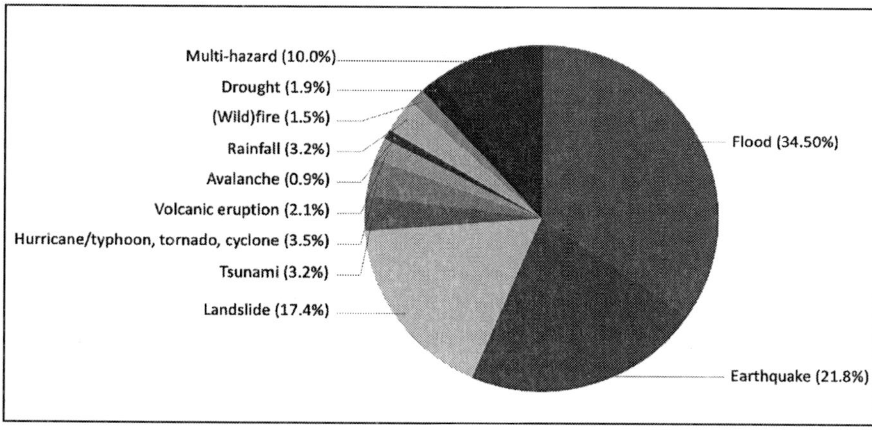

Figure 4.1: Survey of Disaster Risk Reduction

with Intel to map sensitive places and use artificial intelligence to recognize roadways, tunnels, houses, and cities" (*Times of India*, 2019).

A preliminary literature survey including publications published between 2018 and 2021 with a focus on (future) Disaster Risk Reduction (DRR) applications revealed the use of AI to the detection and forecasting of natural hazards and disasters. Certain natural hazards, such as floods, earthquakes, and landslides, are overrepresented in these data. A preliminary literature survey including publications published between 2018 and 2021 with a focus on (future) DRR applications led to the application of AI to the detection and forecasting of natural hazards and disasters. These findings reveal that certain natural hazards, such as floods, earthquakes, and landslides, are overrepresented.

Artificial intelligence (AI), which consists of software algorithms and computer models, is providing new insights into disasters. Artificial intelligence (AI) and satellite data used to identify damaged infrastructure, flooded areas, and roadblocks. For hazard and vulnerability mapping, machine learning commonly employed to detect disaster impact zones. "AI enables the overlaying of several data points with topographic maps (natural resources, heat, and topography). After the 2015, Nepal earthquake humanitarian organisations used community data analysis to get before and after disaster photographs, and machine learning to identify disaster-affected areas (Santhosh Kumar Singh, Ankit Gupta, 2020). Predictive machine learning is also possible thanks to AI. It can be used to analyses seismometer data and create earthquake detection models. This could be useful in the event of a calamity. In the event of a disaster, recovery and response are essential. We are always coming up with new ways to use AI to help with disasters Management. Waveform is an example of invention and earthquake detection analyses processing which improves the detection's precision.

Internet of Things (IoT)

Sensors can offer alerts for potential hazardous situations, allowing the Internet of Things (IoT) to use efficiently for disaster preparedness. "These are real-time integrated systems made possible by the growth of digital infrastructure and software for science and technology, such as computational modeling, sensors, wireless network systems, and machine learning method for data analysis" (Santhosh Kumar Singh, Ankit Gupta 2020). IoT can aid in planning and preparedness by detecting risks via sensors and enabling early warning monitoring, systems that aid in danger mitigation and protection of vital infrastructure, and aid in the deployment of resources in a predictable manner as well as asset tracking and tracing in terms of recovery and responsiveness. It can integrate with GIS for tracking and employ sensors to keep an eye on those involved in rescue activities for example, it can detect the earth's movements, and water levels can be monitored to predict flooding. The Internet of Things (IoT) offers a dynamic method to enhancing productivity. IoT-enabled devices use a lot of power and capable of wireless data transmission. This may make it possible. In the event that network systems fail, communication services are available and encourage catastrophe preparedness. In the same way, an IoT solution can allow for the processing of enormous amounts of data across rivers can be tracked in order to predict floods.

Geological Information System (GIS)

For rescue teams, Geographic Information System is extremely useful. It is a statistical modeling access to use and determine the location of risks with the number of persons affected and also provide appropriate reaction. "Geographic information models and simulation capabilities facilitate decision-makers to both resistance training relief and recovery plans during non-disaster times and also comprehend near real-time possible scenarios, while in an event. Information systems, according to Cutter, can provide crucial social data to aid rescue workers and health authorities to determine majority's susceptibility to a disaster (Arshi ImtiYaz, 2018).

Street Lamps as Innovative Technology

Although street lamps may appear to be an improbable instrument for emergency planning and response but the intelligent street lamps provide a special new layer of functionality to seemingly regular brightness. Weather detectors in these street lamps detect hazards such as increasing water levels, strong winds, extreme heat, and poisonous gas. It also provides a live view of commuter traffic and evolving scenarios with 180-degree cameras. These intelligent street lighting can be used by disaster response organisations to deal with situation and convey vital service to local residents.

Information Communication Technology (ICT)

Emergency services may respond from a variety of places at the scene of a tragedy. In a critical circumstance amount of efficiency technology allowing them to optimise their actions and deliver the best possible response and assist these teams for staying in touch. The School of Information Studies at Northeastern University is developing on a gadget called iDAWG (Intelligent Deployable Augmented Wireless Gateway). This helps to effective machine communication made easier by using this technology. iDAWG can monitor and share signals from a variety of devices, allowing police, firefighters, paramedic teams, local municipalities, and others to connect with each other in the real time. This can serve as a signal repeater for everything from CB bands to private cell phones for bridging the gap between traditional and non-traditional responders.

Drone

Drones can help communities plan for and respond to disasters while also increasing their resilience. Drones can give detailed information over broad areas, while saving time and money. Various organisations have successfully used them to undertake agricultural surveys, notably crop monitoring and verification. Drones can also assist with distant item measuring, which can be useful for planning and rehabilitation projects. "After the 2015 earthquake in Nepal, for example, drones used to produce 3D maps of the devastated areas using image-processing software. This aided in determining the amount of the injury and determining relief and rehabilitation options." Drones have recently been effectively employed during fires, allowing for targeted reaction and securing the lives of firefighters. Thermal sensors installed on drones to locate 'hotspots' and speed up response times. These sensors are also capable of detecting body heat, which can help with post-disaster rescue operations. Drones can also drop aid packages including essential supplies such as food, water, and medicine in remote areas.

Big Data

Flood tags, an integrated digital analytics technology used for screening, graphing, and visualising information based on geography and keywords linked to flood events. Earthquake is a natural calamity that occurs suddenly, and there has been no effective emergency plan for earthquakes until now. However, combining satellite and meteorological data paired with big data analytics can help with earthquake predictions. Through the integration of diverse data formats from many sources, big data can contribute to the early detection of many aspects of floods, such as likely flooding, intensity, and flow velocity. Flood prediction and effect analysis can benefit greatly from both remote sensing and social media data for a faster find the place, time zone, and affected area from the flood and it can combine data from disaster response organisations, remote sensing derived data from the Global Flood Detection System. (Shahinoor Rahman, Liping, D 2017).

Emergency Communication Apps

Now a day's smart phone use is going to be ubiquitous for making these devices excellent for conveying emergency service activities to the public at large. According to a recent study, 68 per cent of mobile phone users at least some of the time use their devices to follow breaking newsworthy events. FEMA has made an app that can help deliver crucial information to at-risk people to see the potential in this trend to assist rescuers had better comprehend the hazard users use the FEMA app to find emergency shelters, weather updates and share their own disaster photographs. The software includes advice on how to deal with more than 20 different types of disasters and calamities. These new and creative response tools can assist public health officials in acting rapidly in the case of an emergency and in the aftermath of an emergency.

Recommendations

Multiple actions are required to provide an ecosystem for the promotion of Disaster Risk Reduction (DRR) technology and developments. These must be oriented toward addressing market creation, customisation, enabling partnerships, and finance issues. The following are some recommendations for enabling such an ecosystem: Create an annual consultation platform for the disaster management community; there are a lot of enterprises and vital investors to engage in discourse.

- Establish and implement a national challenge fund to encourage entrepreneurs to create centres for research and innovation.
- Create a national fund to support the scaling-up of disaster reduction technologies and innovations at the adaptation at global basis stages.
- Establish a well-coordinated supply network that focuses on resolving crisis readiness and responses.
- Develop a digital platform for enhancing disaster risk reduction technology awareness in India to convey on the use of technology in disaster risk management and the transmission of data across numerous key stakeholders.
- Provide financial support at the regional level to encourage entrepreneurs to design and execute recovery and reconstruction technologies and innovations.
- Allow for collaboration in the development and adaptation of new technical solutions for all crisis scenarios.

Conclusion

These technologies can aid model creation and validation, resulting in more effective crisis management. Despite the difficulties, research and data collection on its utility in disaster management are ongoing. Disaster managers and policymakers will have a greater belief in the utility of technology in disaster risk management. These recommendations will allow entrepreneurs to build unique risk assessment and management strategies and technology by providing the necessary adequate funding. The study's findings point to the necessity for partnerships and networks to facilitate interaction among various stakeholder groups in the disaster risk reduction area. This is necessary in order to solve the two most pressing issues: knowledge production and market development for risk and vulnerability mitigation that focuses on technology and innovations. The study aimed to make recommendations that may be highlighted for instant implementation in the medium term to help India develop a recovery and reconstruction ecosystem for survival of all living things.

References

Arshi ImtiYaz (2018) Innovations in disaster risk reduction in India at Oxfam Retrieved from https://www.oxfamindia.org

Atlas Magazine (2020) Natural Disasters in India retrieved from https://www.atlas-mag.net/en/article/natural-disasters-risk-in-India

Carlo Vermgilio, Guido Noto et al. (2021) *Disaster management and emerging technologies: a performance-based perspective* (3) 2049-372X

Gitay, Habiba et al. (2013) Building Resilience: Integrating climate and disaster risk into development. Lessons from World Bank Group experience retrieved from https://www.preventionweb.net

Manish Sharma, Nand Kumar, Ashwani Kumar (2017) Need for Disaster Risk Resilience: A case of India; *International Research Journal of Engineering and Technology* (IRJET), Vol. 4 (11), 2395-0056

Monique Kuglitsch, Arif Albayrak et al. (2022) artificial intelligence disaster risk reduction opportunities challenge, Vol. 71 (1)

Precision Hawk (2018) How Drones Aid in Disaster Response Retrieved from https://www.precisionhawk.com

Santhosh Kumar Singh, Ankit Gupta (2020) Promoting Disaster Risk Resilience Technologies and Innovations in India Guide for Innovators, pp. 9-15

ShahinoorRahman, Liping, D. (2017) The Role of Big Data in Disaster Management retrieved from https://www.researchgate.net/publication/322265557

Statics and data research (2019) retrieved from https://statisticsanddata.org/data/global-deaths-from-natural-disasters

Tae Yoo (2018) Ways technology can play a critical role in disaster response retrieved from https://www.weforum.org/

Times of India (2019) Artificial Intelligence (AI), Internet of things power student projects to manage disasters Retrieved from https://timesofindia.indiamitimes.com

Vinita, Jyoti Gupta, Sangita and Kiran Bala (2016) Disaster Management in India, *International Journal of Humanities and Social Sciences*, Vol. 6, 2250-3226

Williams, R. (2014) "This paper examined the use of Information and communication technologies for disaster risk management in the Caribbean (32) Retrieved from https://repositorio.cepal.org/handle/11362/36735

5

E-Waste – A Gradual National Crisis for India

Paramesh Roy, Eliwon Thiumai, and
Maria Josephine Arokia Marie. S

Introduction

Due to advancements in the field of technology, the electronic industry is booming rapidly and the demand for electronics and electrical appliances is also increasing day by day. Basically, most people do not know about e-waste management. Global e-waste discarded electrical and electronic equipment (EEE) — "will increase by 38 per cent in the decade between 2020 and 2030," according to a new United Nations University (UNU) report (Forti et al., 2020). The dramatic increase on the use of electronic devices leads to increase in disposal of electronic equipment like mobile phones, PCs, refrigerators, air conditioners, personal stereos etc. The use of electronic devices has infiltrated every element of our lives. Despite the positive impact, the negative impact of the electronic waste cannot be underestimated.

There are many factors that contribute to the increase of electronic waste. The changing cultural trends of the use of electronic device that leads to right consumption rates, the gigantic rise in the electronics sector is some of the factors that contribute of the e-waste. As a result, many countries are under pressure to develop and implement environmentally sound e-waste treatment options and practices in order to reduce and to combat the growing environmental and human health hazard posed by e-waste. The development of mechanisms for integrating small unorganised and extensive organisation units into a single value chain is necessary. The sloppy unit can do the extraction, recycling, and disposal of waste, but the organisations have the power to collect, dismantle, and sort out waste. E-waste management is a great challenge for developing countries (Leena, N. et al., 2022). This paper focused that how e-waste management can be handled in our daily lives.

Sarkar (2021) worked on "E-Waste threat and solution to the impending e-waste threat in India with special reference to West Bengal". The main motivation of the work is to understand the threat associated with e-waste and studying the initiative taken by different Government and Non-Government Organisations to find the solution to the impending e-waste threat. Sandhya Balakrishnan (2020) attempted a study on "E-waste management concerns and challenges on the fundamental right to life" mainly focused on to find out a proper mechanism for recycling of e-waste and to provide options to support the decision-making progress for future e-waste management system. Iejse et al., (2020) attempted a study on "E-Waste : A National Health & Environmental Disaster for India". In this paper the researcher attempts to identify each role of the stakeholders regarding e-waste management in detail, government should step forward to increase development of mechanisms regarding e-waste, help of monitoring system etc.

Sivannatham (2020) worked on "Attitude and Skills on E-Waste Management among Undergraduate Students in Thanjavur District". The researcher focused the attitude and the skill development on undergraduate student regarding e-waste management. He used the normative survey method in the study; and variables were attitude and skills. The samples of 210 undergraduate students were collected from different colleges in Thanjavpur district, Tamilnadu. The researcher found that the science stream students were having better knowledge and skill than the arts graduate student. The research concludes that the knowledge and skill of the students are moderated among the whole undergraduate student regarding e-waste management. Shevchenko et al., (2019) focused on the rates of consumer collection of e-waste in their daily lives. The researcher concluded that rates of consumer collection of e-waste depend on the quantity of production.

Al-Rahmi et al., (2018) worked on "Strategies to manage electronic waste approaches: an Overview in East Asia". The researcher introduced the best strategies and techniques to deal with e-waste in East Asia countries. The findings are that the e-waste is increasing in a high level in these countries. Ilankoon et al., (2018) focused on to the future sustainable development of e-waste. And the findings are that the e-waste management systems are having economic improvement by collecting e-waste from the household. Sonu Kumar (2018) conducted on "Teacher's Role in E-Waste Management and Its Impact on the Environment". This is a survey method. To find the role of teachers in e-waste management, the researcher took sample from Dhanbad district, Jharkhand schools for research work. Five schools were selected for gathering sample. After examination, the researcher found that the students, even the teachers, have no proper idea regarding e-waste. Vijarania et al., (2017) investigate the challenge and the effect of e-waste management in developing countries. The findings are that the government should take proper steps to increase development and awareness regarding the e-waste management. Kwatra (2014) found that 12-26 per cent of people replace electronic goods like refrigerators, food processors, personal computers, and other electronic gadgets within the first three years of purchase. The middle-class residents, especially, being unaware of the problem; but, after acquiring the knowledge, they were capable of linking the impacts of improper e-waste management with detrimental health outcomes. The finding of this paper is to develop the customised awareness programmes to address this concern more effectively.

Sivaramanan (2013) analysed the current progress on e-waste management worldwide. He focused on "e-waste management, disposal and its impacts on the environment." The methodology of this paper is theoretical analysis. The research findings revealed that public awareness and manufacturer cooperation are more important for advancements than e-waste management.

A study conducted by Lehtinen et al., (n.d., 2009) examines how the reverse supply chain of Waste Electrical and Electronic Equipment (WEEE) is organised in Finland and Sweden. Second, the paper discusses the structure and efficiency of recovery systems of WEEE based on the literature and the empirical data. It is an explorative in nature and rests on interviews and a real-life experience founded on the three years experiences from Finland. The concluded that the supply chains of WEEE are open-looped so that municipalities, other organisations, and private service providers are responsible for WEEE reverse flow without any involvement of product manufacturers in both Sweden and Finland. The activities of the WEEE recovery business are still an early stage in Finland.

A developing country like India encounters huge problem in generating and managing electronic waste. As a result, our country's e-waste management technique is not effective posing threat to public health and environment. Management of e-waste in India needs to be the approach of holistic.

What is Electronic Waste (E-Waste)?

A wide range of electronic gadgets have outlived their utility and abandoned or outdated by the owners, referred to as e-waste or electronic waste. However, there is no universally accepted definition. Different agencies, on the other hand, have provided varied definitions. E-waste has a high range of rising capabilities of electronic products and from a large number of household equipment such as refrigerators, air conditioners, cell phones, personal stereos, and the consumers' electronic products from the computer that the users had discarded (Garlapati, 2016). Electronic waste commonly known as e-waste or Waste Electrical and Electronic Equipment (WEEE), or end-of-life (EOL) electronic are the electronic appliances such as computers, laptops, TVs, DVD players, mobile phones, MP3 players etc. including their assembly, sub-assembly, components and consumables, which have been disposed of or unwanted by their original users (Bhuie et al., 2004).

Scenario of E-Waste in India

As an IT powerhouse and as a result of modernisation, India has seen an increase in electronic waste, but it is impossible to exactly implement or replicate the e-waste management system due to socio-economic conditions, a lack of infrastructure, a lack of sufficient e-waste legislation, and the strategy and obligations of those engaged. As a result, effective recycling and disposal techniques must be developed in order to reduce environmental pollution and health risks. Heavy metals and halogenated compounds appear to have a major influence on potential health risks (Perkins et al., 2014). In terms of both production and exports, India's electronics industry has emerged as the fastest-growing sector of the Indian economy. E-waste recycling is a severe problem in India because workers in the recycling business are typically underprivileged and illiterate, leaving them fully unaware of the dangers of e-waste. Many women and children who engage in various recycling process among the urban poor are exacerbating the e-waste problem as they are more sensitive to the hazards of this waste material. Dumping of e-waste from some rich countries is one of the primary problems about e-waste, particularly in developing countries such as India and China. Large amounts of discarded electronics are frequently sold to Asia Pacific countries such as India, China, and others. These modern gadgets use a lot of raw materials and have a lot of repair capacity. This can result in enormous accumulations of residue in places where environmental rules are lax. These exports are mostly driven by low labour costs and a lack of environmental and occupational regulations in Asia. As a result, toxic waste from the developed world would flood into the globe's poorest nations (Osibanjo & Nnorom, 2007). In the next 6–8 years, developing countries will produce twice as much e-waste as developed countries (Yu et al., 2010).

By 2030, the developing and developed worlds are expected to trash 400–700 million and 200–300 million old computers, respectively (Garlapati, 2016). E-waste is defined as any trash produced by disposal of electronic gadgets, as well as substances used in their production or use. Because electronic equipment often contains dangerous compounds, disposing of electronics is becoming more difficult. The "Environmental Protection Agency (EPA), more than four million tons of e-waste goes to the U.S. landfills each year". In India, total generated e-waste was 3,32,979 Metric Tonnes (MT) in 2007 [Computer: 56324MT, Mobile Phones: 1655MT, and Televisions: 275000MT] (Chatterjee, 2011). In India, among top

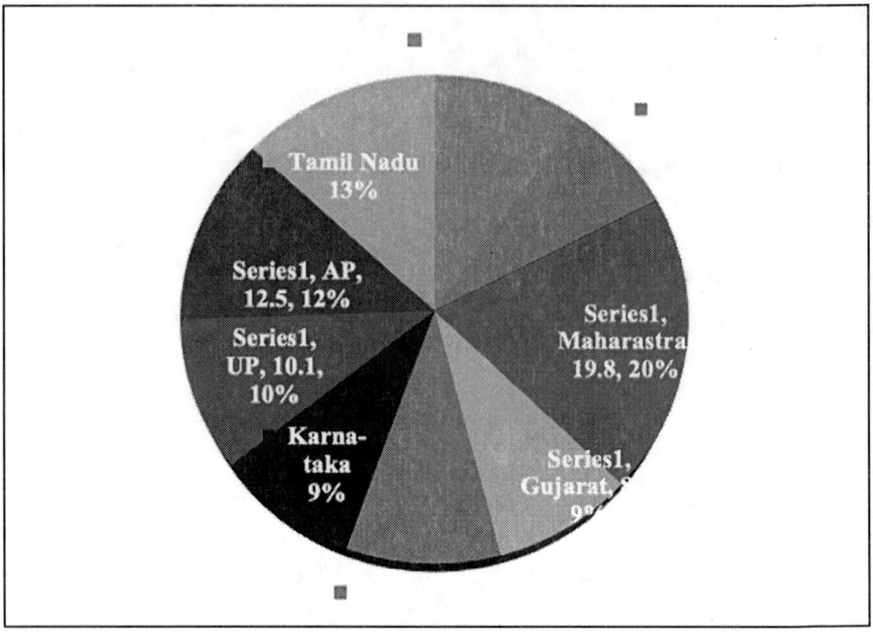

Figure 5.1: State wise E-waste Generation in India (Tonnes/year)

ten cities, Mumbai ranks first in generating e-waste followed by Delhi, Bangalore, Chennai, Kolkata, Ahmadabad, Hyderabad, Pune, Surat and Nagpur (Mathur et al., 2017).

In 2009, the Chilean National Environmental Commission identified Chile as one of the countries with the highest rates of waste generation in Latin America (Wagner et al., 2021). Cambodia (1.10 kg), Vietnam (1.34 kg) and Philippines (1.35 kg) the lowest e-waste generators per capita in 2015 (Latt, 2018). 20-50 million metric tons of e-waste are disposed worldwide every year. But only 17.4 per cent was recycled sustainably (Forti et al., 2020). In India generates about three million tonnes (MT) of e-waste annually and ranks third among e-waste producing countries, after China and the United States. Reports state that it might rise to 5 MT by 2021 (Chatterjee, 2011). Therefore, E-waste is a disaster for health and the environment in the world, and e-waste is a gradual national crisis for India.

Environmental Concerns and Health Hazards

In this modern world of technology everyone uses electronics products such as TV, mobile phone, laptop, computer, AC etc. these electronics product after discarding named as E-waste. E-waste is extremely harmful for people's health. It comprises of several deadly ingredients that are very dangerous to human health and continuously pollute the environment. The presence of highly toxic chemicals in e-waste, such as beryllium, cadmium, mercury, lead, etc., affects the human brain, heart, liver, kidneys, etc. (Karim et al., 2018). Workers and the surrounding community are exposed to harmful substances, such as clastogens and aneugens, due to improper electronic waste (e-waste) processing and disposal. The techniques used in the informal recycling of e-waste, particularly in Lower- and Middle-Income Countries (LMICs), are basic and primitive, with little or no regard for the health and safety of humans and the environment (Issah et al., 2021). The negative consequences of improper e-waste practices disproportionately affect marginalised populations. The "European Commission proposed to revise the directives on electrical and electronic equipment in December 2008 to tackle the increasing volume of waste stream as it was felt that inadequately treated e-waste poses environmental and health risks."

Impact of E-Waste in India

E-Waste is a dangerous element that could spoil our environment. Some of its impacts are discussed below—

- ***Impact on Health:*** As we know, e-waste creates several health problems from toxic chemicals, such as mercury, lead, cadmium, barium, lithium, etc.; these kinds of toxic chemicals affect human health like the brain, heart, liver, kidney, etc. (Ankit et al., 2021).
- ***Impacts on Economy:*** Many companies have economic improvement from e-waste. After the recycling process, the product can be reused and usable to the customer again. This is a profitable business for these companies. The companies buy the e-waste at the cheapest cost, and after furnishing the product, it is sold by the companies at a reasonable cost (Awasthi et al., 2019).

Table 5.1: E-waste appliances, Toxic Ingredients and its Effect on Human Health and Environment

E-Waste Appliances/ Gadgets/Equipments	*Contain Toxic Ingredients*	*Effect on Human Health and Environment*
Mobile Phone	Lead, Mercury, Beryllium	Discarded mobile phones contain chemicals such as lead, mercury, beryllium which causes cancer, neurological and developmental disorder (Karim et al., 2018).
Fridge	CFC (Chloro-fluorocarbon)	CFC (Chlorofluorocarbon) released from fridge causes skin cancer (Pollut et al., 2022).
TV	Lead, Mercury and Beryllium	Lead, Mercury and Beryllium released from TV causes shortness of breath, headache and chest pain (Patel, 2015).
Monitors and Processors	Toxic Dusts	Monitors and processors contain residual toxic dusts that are linked to various reproductive and neurological problems (Karim et al., 2018).
LED	Lead and Mercury	Lead and mercury ejected from LED causes damage to our eyes and skin (Scheer, 2018).
Coffee Makers	Toxic Fungi	Discarded coffee makers develop toxic fungi that is hazardous to our health (Siri-Anusornsak, 2022).
LCD display and Computer Chips	Arsenic Oxide	Arsenic oxide present in circuit boards, LCD display and computer chips causes skin and lung cancer (Patel, 2015).
AC	HCFC (Hydrochloro-fluorocarbon)	Hydrochlorofluorocarbons (HCFCs) released from leakage of AC can destroy the earth's protective ozone layer (US Environmental Protection Agency, 2020).

- ***Impacts on Environment:*** E-waste exhales the heat of toxic chemicals that affect our atmosphere and create global warming, affecting soil, water, etc. (Rao, 2014).

Future Recommendations for Indian Scenario

- ***Cost of Essential Products:*** Such as Labour cost, transporting cost, processing cost, etc. They are essential for the recycling process (Perera et al., 1999). Many organisations are afraid of this cost and do not want to go for the recycling process of e-waste management. The low cost of such essential products can reduce the problem.
- ***Development of Mechanisms:*** In developing an e-waste management system, the mechanical procedure is the main process. That is why the development of mechanisms is also needed. Like other countries, our country is not as good as in mechanical progress. The development of mechanisms can help to develop e-waste management (Wath et al., 2010).
- ***Spreading Network:*** The organisation should have a list of NGOs and have a network associated with e-waste management could help the organisation to have help regarding the e-waste management system. They also serve the materials that should be essential for managing e-waste (Pedro et al., 2021).
- ***Promoting Awareness Regarding Environment-Friendly Disposal:*** NGOs and organisations should organise seminars, and webinars, regarding the promotion of eco-friendly disposal. The above decision taken by the organisations should help them and can be profitable (Widmer et al., 2005). And they also provide the treatments or disposal regarding e-waste.

Conclusion

Originally emerged from advanced countries, e-waste is the fastest-growing sort of waste, and now expanding to developing nations like India. Innovative technologies in the development of electronic equipment contribute to rapid degradation, resulting in substantial e-waste generation. For developing countries like India, e-waste management is a mammoth task. As a result, it is complicated because there are not any strict standards or regulations in place to manage the massive amount of e-waste generated. One way to reduce e-waste is to set stringent regulations and impose heavy fines on industries that do not comply with the regulations. Without a doubt, in many developed countries, e-waste recycling has become a non-viable business. However, the volume of e-waste is increasing dramatically. Toxic substances in e-waste are extremely dangerous to humans. As a result, a holistic approach to resolving this issue must be given due consideration.

References

Al-Rahmi, W., Alias, N., Ali, A., Yahaya, N., Saleh, M., & Al-Maatouk, Q. (2018). Strategies to manage electronic waste approaches: An overview in east Asia. *International Journal of Engineering and Technology (UAE)*, *7*(4), 3268–3275. https://doi.org/10.14419/ijet.v7i4.15169

Ankit, Saha, L., Kumar, V., Tiwari, J., Sweta, Rawat, S., Singh, J., & Bauddh, K. (2021). Electronic waste and their leachates impact on human health and environment: Global ecological threat and management. *Environmental Technology and Innovation*, *24*(December), 102049. https://doi.org/10.1016/j.eti.2021.102049

Awasthi, A.K., Li, J., Koh, L., & Ogunseitan, O.A. (2019). Circular economy and electronic waste. *Nature Electronics*, *2*(3), 86–89. https://doi.org/10.1038/s41928-019-0225-2

Bhuie, A.K., Ogunseitan, O.A., Saphores, J.D.M., & Shapiro, A.A. (2004). Environmental and economic trade-offs in consumer electronic products recycling: A case study of cell phones and computers. *IEEE International Symposium on Electronics and the Environment*, *June*, 74–79. https://doi.org/10.1109/isee.2004.1299691

Chatterjee, S. (2011). *Electronic Waste and India*. 1–15. www.greenpeace.org

E-Waste Management — Concerns and Challenges on the Fundamental Right to Life Thesis submitted to the SNDT Women's University in partial fulfilment of the requirements for the Award of the Degree of Ph.D. In Law By Sandhya Balakrishnan Under the supe. (2020).

Forti, V., Baldé, C.P., Kuehr, R., & Bel, G. (2020). The Global E-waste Monitor 2020: Quantities, Flows, and the Circular Economy Potential. In United Nations University (UNU)/United Nations Institute for Training and Research (UNITAR) – co-hosted SCYCLE Programme, International Telecommunication Union (ITU) & International Solid Waste Association (ISWA), Bonn/Geneva/Rotterdam. https://collections.unu.edu/view/UNU:7737#.YmFDOI2v_Hs.mendeley

Garlapati, V.K. (2016). E-waste in India and developed countries: Management, recycling, business and biotechnological initiatives. *Renewable and Sustainable Energy Reviews*, *54*, 874–881. https://doi.org/10.1016/j.rser.2015.10.106

Iejse, E., Arya, S., Gupta, A., & Bhardwaj, A. (2020). *International Educational Journal Of Science And E-Waste – A National Health & Environmental Disaster For India.* December 2018, 26–33.

Ilankoon, I.M.S.K., Ghorbani, Y., Chong, M.N., Herath, G., Moyo, T., & Petersen, J. (2018). E-waste in the international context – A review of trade flows, regulations, hazards, waste management strategies and technologies for value recovery. *Waste Management, 82*, 258–275. https://doi.org/10.1016/j.wasman.2018.10.018

Issah, I., Arko-mensah, J., Agyekum, T.P., Dwomoh, D., & Fobil, J.N. (2021). *Electronic waste exposure and DNA damage : a systematic review and meta-analysis.*

Karim, S.M.R., Sharif, S.I., & Anik, A.R. (2018). *Negative Impact and Probable Management Policy of E-Waste in Bangladesh.* 1–6.

Kwatra, S. (2014). *Understanding public knowledge and awareness on e-waste in an urban setting in India A case study for Delhi. 25*(6), 752–765. https://doi.org/10.1108/MEQ-12-2013-0139

Latt, H. (2018). *E-Waste Management in Myanmar.*

Leena, N.M., Mayur S., N., & Prabhakar R., P. (2022). Current Practices of Management/Handling of E-waste: A Review. *International Journal of Zoological Investigations, 08*(01), 55–61. https://doi.org/10.33745/ijzi.2022.v08i01.008

Lehtinen, U., Poikela, K., Ylä-mella, J., & Pongrácz, E. (n.d.). *Examining The Weee Recovery Supply Chain.* 517–531.

Mathur, A., Choudhari, A., Yadav, P.S., & Murari, K. (2017). Experimental Study of Concrete using Combination of EWaste and Plastic Waste as Coarse Aggregate. *International Journal of Civil Engineering, 4*(5), 36–39. https://doi.org/10.14445/23488352/ijce-v4i5p109

Osibanjo, O., & Nnorom, I.C. (2007). The challenge of electronic waste (e-waste) management in developing countries. *Waste Management and Research, 25*(6), 489–501. https://doi.org/10.1177/0734242X07082028

Patel, B.N. (2015). *Issn . 2278-6236 E Waste Problems an Analysis Issn : 2278-6236. 4*(7), 60–71.

Pedro, F., Giglio, E., Contreras, L.V., & Munguia, N. (2021). Constructed governance as solution to conflicts in e-waste recycling networks. *Sustainability (Switzerland), 13*(4), 1–22. https://doi.org/10.3390/su13041701

Perera, H.S.C., Nagarur, N., & Tabucanon, M.T. (1999). Component part standardization: a way to reduce the life-cycle costs of products. *International Journal of Production Economics, 60*(February), 109–116. https://doi.org/10.1016/S0925-5273(98)00179-0

Perkins, D.N., Drisse, M.B., Nxele, T., & Sly, P.D. (2014). E-Waste : A Global Hazard. *Annals of Global Health*, *80*(4), 286–295. https://doi.org/10.1016/j.aogh.2014.10.001

Pollut, E., Change, C., & Xu, H. (2022). *Environment Pollution and Climate Change What Effects do Chlorofluorocarbons Have on Humans ?* *6*(3), 3–4.

Rao, L.N. (2014). Environmental impact of uncontrolled disposal of e-wastes. *International Journal of ChemTech Research*, *6*(2), 1343–1353.

Sarkar, T. (2021). E-Waste threat and solution to the impending e-waste threat in India with special reference to West Bengal. *IISRR-International Journal of Research*, *7*(August). http://goaspcb.gov.in

SCHEER. (2018). Opinion on potential risks to human health of light emitting diodes (LEDs). In *Scientific Committee on Health, Environmental and Emerging Risks (SCHEER)* (Issue June).

Shevchenko, T., Laitala, K., & Danko, Y. (2019). Understanding consumer e-waste recycling behavior: Introducing a new economic incentive to increase the collection rates. *Sustainability (Switzerland)*, *11*(9). https://doi.org/10.3390/su11092656

Siri-Anusornsak. (2022). *The Occurrence and Co-Occurrence of Regulated, Emerging, and Masked Mycotoxins in Rice Bran and Maize from Southeast Asia. 14*(8), 1–18. https://doi.org/10.3390/%0Atoxins14080567

Sivannatham, R. n. d. (2020). Attitude And Skills On E- Waste Management Among Undergraduate Students. *Dogo Rangsang Research Journal, UGC Care Group I Journal*, *10*(11), 19–26. https://www.journal-dogorangsang.in/no_1_nov_20/2.pdf

Sivaramanan, S. (2013). E-Waste Management, Disposal and Its Impacts on the Environment. *Universal Journal of Environmental Research and Technology www.environmentaljournal.Org*, *3*(5), 531–537. http://www.environmentaljournal.org/3-5/ujert-3-5-1.pdf

Sonu Kumar. (2018). Teacher'S Role in E-Waste Management and Its Impact on the Environment. *IMPACT: International Journal of Research in Humanities, Arts and Literature (IMPACT: IJRHAL)*, *6*(2), 249–256. http://www.impactjournals.us/archives.php?year=2018_11_2&id=11&jtype=2&page=7

US Environmental Protection Agency. (2020). Phasing Out HCFC Refrigerants To Protect The Ozone Layer. *U.S. Environmental Protection Agency*, 1–2. https://www.epa.gov/sites/production/files/2015-07/documents/phasing_out_hcfc_refrigerants_to_protect_the_ozone_layer.pdf

Vijarania, M., Gupta, S., & Gambhir, A. (2017). Challenges and strategies for E-waste management in developing countries. *IJ Sci. Eng.*, *2*(9), 64–68. http://

oaijse.com/VolumeArticles/FullTextPDF/79_OAIJSE_CHALLENGES_AND_STRATEGIES_FOR_E-WASTE_MANAGEMENT_IN_DEVELOPING_COUNTRIES_13.pdf

Wagner, M., Luda, V., Nnorom, I.C., Kuehr, R., & Iattoni, G. (2021). *E-WASTE MONITOR*.

Wath, S.B., Vaidya, A.N., Dutt, P.S., & Chakrabarti, T. (2010). A roadmap for development of sustainable E-waste management system in India. *Science of the Total Environment*, *409*(1), 19–32. https://doi.org/10.1016/j.scitotenv.2010.09.030

Widmer, R., Oswald-Krapf, H., Sinha-Khetriwal, D., Schnellmann, M., & Böni, H. (2005). Global perspectives on e-waste. *Environmental Impact Assessment Review*, *25*(5 SPEC. ISS.), 436–458. https://doi.org/10.1016/j.eiar.2005.04.001

Yu, J., Williams, E., Ju, M., & Yang, Y. (2010). Forecasting global generation of obsolete personal computers. *Environmental Science and Technology*, *44*(9), 3232–3237. https://doi.org/10.1021/es903350q

6

Awareness of Disaster Risk Reduction

Study of Higher Secondary Students at Tiruchirappalli

C. Hariharan

Introduction

According to Disaster Risk Reduction (DRR) in India (2020) report, India has shown different type of sudden and slow-onset natural hazards, from hydro meteorological threats, for example landslides, flooding, droughts, cyclones and earthquakes, extreme temperature to wildfires, and epidemics. Also, vulnerability may build from anthropogenic sources when creatures (like as person, animals, birds etc.) are the possible to be unsuccessful. Disasters never affect population groups equally. A lot, their effects are spread in socio-economic, wherein hierarchies of power, marginalisation, uneven sharing of services, or bias influence an individual's skills and capacity to cope with external shocks. Some of the factors such as gender, age, religion, caste, and ethnicity may give to one's poverty and vulnerability in social context (Perwaiz et al., 2020).

Mamon et al. (2017) stated that effective disaster risk reduction education is vital in the fundamental education curriculum, freeze and make the attentiveness to strengthen the culture, preparedness, mitigation, prevention, adaptation, and resiliency among the pupils. Apronti (2015) revealed that the most of disaster vulnerable victims have risks and affect the physical, emotional, and psychological well-being. Baker et al., (2015) examine the disaster education aims and to enhance the resiliency of students on disaster risk reduction by consolidating awareness about disasters, improving skills that can be utilised to adapt, prepare, mitigate, and react to the damaging effects of disasters, and inspiring attentiveness that widens the scope of awareness on disaster risk reduction. Asharose et al., (2015) explained in their study the objectives of disaster risk reduction; this is advocated by increasing safety culture and resiliency in the society, particularly at the school level. In this way, the researcher involved to find out the higher secondary students' awareness of disaster risk reduction.

Review of Literature

Gampell et al., (2020) recommended video games as a modern teaching method to engage geography students. They framed a constructive learning theory-based video games programme for the students. The findings of the study revealed that the use of video games inside the school involved additional consideration of the teaching and learning processes for both teachers and students. Winarni and Purwandari (2018) reported that there is a need to provide knowledge about the earthquake disaster mitigation, especially in elementary school, and to grow the "Safety Culture" in school. The educational mobile application influences the students understanding about earthquake disaster preparedness. The mobile learning application is one of the effective tools for earthquake education, because it gives the earthquake information in more interactive manner. Kamil et al., (2020) finding revealed that there was an increase of knowledge and understanding of students by using through geographic literacy in student learning on the material of disaster-related theme. So, teachers were expected to use teaching materials based on geographical perspective to support learning of disaster risk reduction. In that way, students who were aware of disaster risk reduction strategies could help to save the country from natural hazards.

Materials and Methods

Participants

There were six schools from Tiruchirappalli district randomly selected using simple random sampling technique for collecting data. The data was collected from 403 higher secondary students in diverge disciplines from the six schools with two each of Government, Aided and Self-financing categories. The aided schools are private schools with the grant in aid from the government whereas Self-financing schools are private schools with no grant in aid from the government. The key sub-group of the participants are 168 (41.69%) higher secondary students from government schools; 111 (27.54%) from aided schools and 124 (30.77) from self-financing. Participants were male students (51.36 per cent) and female students (48.63%). 47.15 per cent were from a science discipline (Physics, Chemistry, Mathematics, Botany, Zoology, etc.) and 52.85 per cent were from arts discipline (Economics, Commerce, History, Language, etc.). Based on locality of the participants from rural (39.1%), urban (14.9%) were chosen.

Procedure

This research study had utilised to design as cross-sectional method in which it tries to assess the perception of disaster, vigilance and readiness, adaptation, awareness, and risk perception of higher secondary students who are studying in eleventh standard. A simple random sampling technique was utilised to obtain 403 respondents from four schools at Tiruchirappalli district in India. All of the information gathered in this type of survey should always be compared to the social norms for the group being surveyed and tested. Data collection was done in January and February 2022. Schools in the selected regions were approached for participation in the research. They were asked to answer the "Awareness of Disaster Risk Reduction Inventory for Students". Average completion time for each survey was approximately twenty minutes.

Materials

The survey consisted of two parts. In the first part, participants gave their informed consent and provided background information about their gender (e.g., Male and Female), type of school they studied (Government, Aided, Unaided) studying discipline (Science — Physics, Chemistry, Mathematics, Botany, Zoology; and Arts — Economics, Commerce, Language etc.), locality of the students' home (Rural and Urban).

In the second part, participants completed the "Awareness of Disaster Risk Reduction Inventory for Students". The tool was developed by the researcher. The researchers got idea of the statements from various previous studies (for examples Gampell, et al., 2020; Kamil et al., 2020; Winarni and Purwandari, 2018; Mamon et al. 2017; Apronti, 2015; Asharose et al., 2015; Baker et al., 2015). There were two main phases, such as content validity and factor analysis conducted during the tool development of "Awareness of Disaster Risk Reduction Inventory for Students". The participants were to respond by making one of five options: "Strongly Agree" (5) to "No Idea" (1). Scoring is provided as, "Strongly Agree" (5), "Agree" (4) "Strongly Disagree" (3), "Disagree" (2) and "No Idea" (1) for each statement.

A pilot study was conducted among the thirty higher secondary students in Tiruchirappalli region. The gathered data were processed through an SPSS 16.0 for the factor analysis. Factor analysing value must be 0.7 or more (Salkind, 2010). As a result of the first factor analysis, fifteen items were removed from the inventory because their factor levels were not as high as required (0.7). After, the 20 items were considered as a final version of the inventory, which is also divided five dimensions as, namely: 1) Perception of Disaster, 2) Disaster vigilance and readiness, 3) Disaster adaptation, 4) Disaster awareness, and 5) Disaster risk perception. All the statements were consisted by the awareness of disaster risk management and the students' readiness. Each dimension has four statements.

Data Analysis

The data was analysed using an SPSS (Statistical Package for the Social Sciences) version 16.0 for windows. The α value for all statistical tests was set to 0.05. To examine the awareness of disaster risk management to practise or perceive in society among the higher secondary students, at the analysis was conducted with the percentage of the respondent answers to the general assertions as the dependent variable. Before the analysis, Cronbach's Alpha was utilised to find out whether the inventory in the context of research has reliable or not. The reliability of the tool value is 0.842 which indicates that the inventory was observed to display high alpha scores.

Results

Analysis and interpretation of the result is the most important steps after the data collection. The collected data has been analysed using the descriptive analysis.

Descriptive Analysis

Descriptive analysis summarises the data meaningfully. It is used to measure the percentage of variation in the awareness towards disaster risk management among the higher secondary students. Based on the scores obtained by them in "Awareness of Disaster Risk Reduction Inventory for Students" that was intended to measure their awareness of disaster risk management.

The above table 6.1 summarised proportion of (Likert scale 1-5 such as Strongly Agree, Agree, Strongly Disagree, Disagree and No Idea) responses for each Awareness of Disaster Risk Reduction (DRR) statements. For the overall sample, a very few responded that is 2 per cent not having any idea about the Disaster Risk Reduction. Also, 9 per cent used disagree. 18 per cent used Strongly Disagree. 34 per cent agreed to manage the disaster risk reduction. A total of responded (37%) sturdily agreed to manage the disaster risk reduction in Awareness of Disaster Risk Reduction Inventory for Students' statements. An analysis of the responses for each statement showed a lot of variation in the awareness towards disaster risk reduction. Two of the 20 awareness statements were strongly agreed to utilise and practise by the students, more than 66 per cent of higher secondary students. The most responded of these disaster risk reduction awareness statements (6) "I know the vital role of making conversations about disasters with family members, friends, neighbours, and relatives." and (8) "I am sure that reform activities can be implemented after disaster" were strongly agreed (66.25%). The above obtained result clearly indicates that higher secondary students as many as 37 per cent were found to have a high-level awareness of disaster risk reduction. Unless the people are high in their awareness of disaster risk reduction, they shall be too young to win the disaster in their place.

Findings

1. The overall level of awareness towards the disaster risk reduction among the higher secondary students is average.
2. The dimension of disaster related knowledge reveal that students need to participate in disaster management training.

Table 6.1: Level of Awareness towards Disaster Risk Reduction in Percentage

S. No.	Statements	Strongly Agree	Agree	Strongly Disagree	Disagree	No Idea
	Perception of Disaster					
1	I understand when a disaster will happen	34.00	35.98	8.44	12.41	9.18
2	I understand where a disaster will happen	41.44	33.50	7.20	6.70	11.17
3	I know how to prevent the occurrence of disaster	31.51	27.54	20.35	18.86	1.74
4	I have participated in a disaster management training	5.71	3.23	41.69	49.13	0.25
	Disaster Vigilance and Readiness					
5	I know the significance of sharing my experiences and information about disaster	58.81	37.22	2.98	0.50	0.50
6	I know the vital role of making conversations about disasters with family members, friends, neighbours, and relatives.	66.25	31.02	0.25	0.74	1.74
7	I know how the government is ready to provide assistance after disaster	45.91	34.49	11.17	5.96	2.48
8	I am sure that reform activities can be implemented after disaster	66.25	31.76	1.24	0.74	0.00
	Disaster Adaptation					
9	I am aware about which government organisation needs to be coordinated and contacted with after disaster	34.24	30.02	27.05	5.96	2.73
10	I am informed about disaster prone areas	31.51	32.51	21.34	12.90	1.74
11	I obtained sufficient information about disaster adaptation from the local government or from NGOs	34.49	40.94	14.14	9.18	1.24
12	I am aware about the evacuation system and plan in my locality, or area	33.25	30.77	19.35	16.38	0.25

	Disaster Awareness					
13	I actively participate for disaster awareness campaigns	41.69	29.03	22.33	6.95	0.00
14	I am prepared with emergency kits and bags in case of disaster	26.05	36.72	19.35	15.88	1.99
15	I prioritise awareness on the local, regional, and national level	24.57	40.94	19.60	14.14	0.74
16	I am aware on the importance of building or infrastructure retrofitting	34.00	38.46	26.05	1.24	0.25
	Disaster Risk Perception					
17	I am sure that large-scale disasters will happen certainly in the next ten years	14.14	41.44	30.02	8.19	6.20
18	I think my locality is safe from all types of disasters	16.63	21.59	31.51	27.54	2.73
19	I think my house/building is well designed to withstand an earthquake	26.80	30.02	22.08	14.64	6.45
20	I think my family members always followed mask wearing, social distance, sanitizer during the Covid-19 period.	32.75	36.23	21.84	7.94	1.24
	Total	37	34	18	9	2

3. The dimension of disaster preparedness and readiness indicate that the higher secondary students want to improve their awareness about the government provide assistance after disaster.
4. The dimension of disaster adaptation justify that the higher secondary students have low level of awareness in this area.
5. The dimension of disaster awareness reveals that most of the student not prepared with emergency kits and bags for disaster.
6. The dimension of disaster risk perception indicate that majority of students didn't know their locality is safe from all types of disasters.

Conclusion

The research proves the importance of school systems in improving disaster risk management. Higher secondary pupils must be aware of some concepts of disaster related to preparedness, adapted, ideas and aware on the risks inflicted by these natural hazards. Low awareness on disaster risks are evidently observed among higher secondary pupils. The pupils' responses could be based on the competence and impact of the integration of disaster risk reduction education in the higher secondary curriculum. In particular, incorporation of the concepts about the knowledge of disaster, preparedness, mitigation, prevention, adaptation, hazards, hazard maps and resiliency in the science curriculum possibly affect the understanding awareness of pupils on disaster risk reduction. In this context, the continuous growth of disaster risk reduction education at all stages of the educational process, beginning with higher secondary schools, is required. The school curriculum ought to include the theoretical background and practical experience in health protection. In addition, this research focused on how to influence the students' awareness toward improved disaster risk reduction. Consequently, the researcher suggests that future studies focus on the role of educational stakeholders in enhancing disaster risk reduction awareness in educational curriculum.

References

Apronti P.T, Osamu S, Otsuki K, and Berisavljevic G.K. (2015). Education for disaster risk reduction (DRR): Linking theory with practice in Ghana's basic schools. Retrieved from: http:// www.mdpi.com/2071-1050/7/7/9160.

Asharose, Saizen, I, Sasi, P.K. (2015). Awareness workshop as an effective tool and approach for education in disaster risk reduction: A case study from Tamil Nadu, India. Sustainability Vol.7, pp-8965-84. Retrieved from: http://www.mdpi.com.

Baker O.E., Kasapoglu, K. and Yilmaz, E. (2015). The objectives of disaster education from teachers' perspectives. *International Journal of Human Science*, Vol.12, pp-975-90. Retrieved from: https://www.j-humansciences.com/ojs/index.php/IJHS/article/ view/3196/1457.

Gampell, A., Gaillard, J.C., Parsons, M., & Le Dé, L. (2020). 'Serious' disaster video games: An innovative approach to teaching and learning about disasters and disaster risk reduction. *Journal of geography*, *119*(5), 159-170. Retrieved from: https://doi.org/10.1080/00221341.2020.1795225

Kamil, P.A., Utaya, S., & Utomo, D.H. (2020). Improving disaster knowledge within high school students through geographic literacy. *International journal of disaster risk reduction*, *43*, 101411. Retrieved from: https://doi.org/10.1016/j.ijdrr.2019.101411

Mamon, M.A.C., Suba, R.A.V., & Son, I.L. (2017). Disaster risk reduction knowledge of Grade 11 students: Impact of senior high school disaster education in the Philippines. *International Journal of Health System and Disaster Management*, *5*(3), 69.

Perwaiz, A., Parviainen, J., Somboon, P. and Mcdonald, A., (2020). *Disaster Risk Reduction in India.* Retrieved from: https://www.undrr.org/media/48528/download

Salkind, N.J. (2010). Encyclopedia of research design Thousand Oaks, CA: *SAGE Publications*, Inc. Retrieved from doi: 10.4135/9781412961288

Winarni, E.W. & Purwandari, E.P. (2018). Disaster risk reduction for earthquake using mobile learning application to improve the students understanding in elementary school. *Mediterranean Journal of Social Sciences*, *9*(2), 205. Retrieved from: http://archive.sciendo.com/MJSS/mjss.2018.9.issue-2/mjss-2018-0040/mjss-2018-0040.pdf

7

Climate Change and Environmental Problems
Students' Perception in Tiruchirappalli

R. Praveena and M. Mirunalini

Introduction

Climate change is the long-term alteration of temperature and typical weather patterns in a place. Climate change could refer to a particular location or the planet as a whole. Climate change may cause weather patterns to be less predictable. These unexpected weather patterns can make it difficult to maintain and grow crops in regions that rely on farming because expected temperature and rainfall levels can no longer be relied on. Climate change has also been connected with other damaging weather events such as more frequent and more intense hurricanes, floods, downpours, and winter storms.

"Climate change" and "global warming" are often used interchangeably but have distinct meanings. Similarly, the terms "weather" and "climate" are sometimes confused, though they refer to events with broadly different spatial — and timescales. Scientists use observations from the ground, air, and space, along with computer models, to monitor and study past, present, and future climate change. Climate data records provide evidence of climate change key indicators, such as global land and ocean temperature increases; rising sea levels; ice loss at Earth's poles and in mountain glaciers;

frequency and severity changes in extreme weather such as hurricanes, heat waves, wildfires, droughts, floods, and precipitation; and cloud and vegetation cover changes.

Climate change includes both global warming driven by human-induced emissions of greenhouse gases and the resulting large-scale shifts in weather patterns.

Though there have been previous periods of climatic change, since the mid-20th century humans have had an unprecedented impact on Earth's climate system and caused change on a global scale

- Climate change is a periodic modification of earth's climate brought about due to the changes in the atmosphere as well as the interactions between the atmosphere and various other geological, chemical, biological and geographical factors within the earth's system.
- Climate change can make weather patterns less predictable. These unforeseen weather patterns can make it difficult to maintain and grow crops, making agriculture-dependent countries like India vulnerable.
- It is also causing damaging weather events like more frequent and intense hurricanes, floods, cyclones, flooding etc.
- Due to the rising temperature caused by climate change, the ice in the polar regions is melting at an accelerated rate, causing sea levels to rise. This is damaging the coastlines due to the increased flooding and erosion.
- The cause of the current rapid climate change is due to human activities and threatening the very survival of humankind.
- The largest driver of warming is the emission of gases that create a greenhouse effect, of which more than 90 per cent are carbon dioxide (CO2) and methane.
- Fossil fuel burning (coal, oil, and natural gas) for energy consumption is the main source of these emissions, with additional contributions from agriculture, deforestation, and manufacturing.
- Temperature rise is accelerated or tempered by climate feedbacks, such as loss of sunlight-reflecting snow and ice cover, increased water vapour (a greenhouse gas itself), and changes to land and ocean carbon sinks.

- Temperature rise on land is about twice the global average increase, leading to desert expansion and more common heat waves and wildfires.
- Temperature rise is also amplified in the Arctic, where it has contributed to melting permafrost, glacial retreat and sea ice loss.
- Warmer temperatures are increasing rates of evaporation, causing more intense storms and weather extremes.
- Impacts on ecosystems include the relocation or extinction of many species as their environment changes, most immediately in coral reefs, mountains, and the Arctic.
- Climate change threatens people with food insecurity, water scarcity, flooding, infectious diseases, extreme heat, economic losses, and displacement.
- These human impacts have led the World Health Organization to call climate change the greatest threat to global health in the 21st century.
- Even if efforts to minimise future warming are successful, some effects will continue for centuries, including rising sea levels, rising ocean temperatures, and ocean acidification.

Tiruchirappalli, situated on the banks of the river Cauvery is the fourth largest city in Tamil Nadu. It was a citadel of the early Cholas which later fell to the Pallavas. Trichy is a fine blend of tradition and modernity built around the Rock Fort. Apart from the Fort, there are several Temples dating back to the 1760s. The town and its fort, now in Trichy were built by the Nayaks of Madurai. This District has given great scholars and leaders whose contributions to the society have been very significant. This study intends to know the students' perception on climate change and various environment issues related to the Tiruchirappalli District of Tamil Nadu.

Materials and Methods

Methods

Normative survey method was employed for the present study. The sample size for the present study is 94. Out of ninety-four (94) samples, 68 were undergraduate and 24 were postgraduate students (21 males and

73 females). Students' perception on climate change and Environmental Issues questionnaire were used for the data collection.

Result and Discussion

From the above table, it was found that 55.4 per cent responded that climate change affected their life, 72.3 per cent responded that global temperature were increasing, 82.9 per cent felt that rainfall is decreasing due to climate change, 87.2 per cent felt that climate change is a real problem in Tiruchirappalli, 86.1 per cent felt that climate change causing deadly diseases like Covid-19 and 71.2 per cent felt that global warming be the biggest problem in the future.

From that table it was found that, 87 per cent responded that overpopulation is the cause for environmental problems in Trichy, 84 per cent responded

Table7. 1: Students Perception on Climate Change in Percentage

S. No.	*Statement*	*Respondent (Yes) %*	*Respondent (NO) %*
1	Do you feel Climate change affected your life	55.4	44.6
2	Are global temperature rising	72.3	27.7
3	Do you feel rainfall decreasing is occurring	82.9	17.1
4	Do you feel climate change is a real problem in Tiruchirappalli	87.2	12.8
5	Is climate change causing deadly diseases like Covid-19	86.1	13.9
6	Will global warming be the biggest problem in the future	71.2	28.8

Table 7. 2: Causes for Environmental Problems of Tiruchirappalli

Causes Environmental Problems	*Percentage*
Overpopulation	87
Air pollution	65
Deforestation	74
Climate change	84
Noise pollution	35

that climate change is the cause, 74 per cent felt deforestation is the cause, 65 per cent responded that air pollution is the cause for environmental problems in Trichy.

Conclusion

Higher education plays a vital role in educating citizens about climate change and promoting pro-environment behaviour. Since when the climate change was being accepted as one of the most important issues of the new century, individuals' behaviour, perceptions, knowledge and awareness in relation to climate change mitigation and adaptation started to be the focus of research studies. Students' understanding and awareness on environmental issues such as climate change are vital for development of an understanding in larger scale especially when younger generations are in question.

References

Bhowmik Roy, S.K. and Das, Ananda K. (2007.June). Rainfall analysis for Indian monsoon region using the merged rain gauge observations and satellite estimates: Evaluation of monsoon rainfall features, J. Earth Syst. Sci. 116(3), 187-198.

Campbell, E., Skovdal, M., and Campbell. (2013). Ethiopian Students' Relationship with their Environment: Implications for Environmental and Climate Adaptation Programmes, Children's Geographies, 11: 4, 436-460.

CCC&AR and TNSCCC (2015). Climate Change Projection (Temperature) for Tiruchirappalli. URL. www.tnsccc.in

Climate Change and India. (2008). Impacts, policy responses and a framework for EU-India cooperation. Policy Department Economic and Scientific Policy, European Parliament. 34. National action plan on climate change. (2009). Accessed on 21.8.2012, http://moef.nic.in/downloads/others/CC_ghosh.pdf

Hans C. Ossebaard, Peter lachman (2020) Climate change, environmental sustainability and health care quality. *International Journal for Quality in Health Care*, 33(1)1-3. doi: 10.1093/intqhc/mzaa036

Hope. K.R., (2009). Climate Change and Poverty in Africa, *International Journal of Sustainable Development and World Ecology*, 16: 6, 451-461. http://ecourts.gov.in/tn/tiruchirappalli http://www.tiruchirappalli.nic.in/trichynew/district/distnew.html

Mengistu, D.K., (2011). Farmers' Perception and Knowledge of Climate Change and their Coping Strategies to the Related Hazardous: Case Study from Adiha, Central Tigray, Ethiopia, Agricultural Science 2:2, 138-145.

Ministry of Environment and Forests, Government of India. (2010). INCCA: Indian network for climate change assessment report; climate change and India, A 4x4 assessment: A sectoral and regional analysis for 2030.

UNFCCC. United Nations Framework Convention on Climate Change https://www.google.com/url?sa=t&source=web&rct=j&url=https://unfccc.int/files/essential_background/background_publications_htmlpdf/application/pdf/conveng.pdf&ved=2ahUKEwj9s73a_In6AhV_3zgGHTVTAO8QFnoECFEQBQ&usg=AOvVaw0sg_BvpAJzwfzg1nyV_jwt

World Health Organization https://www.who.int/globalchange/global campaign/cop21/en/. (27 January 2020, date last accessed)

8

Ecological Tribal World View
A Solution for Climate Resilience

Rakesh Kumar

Introduction

For sustainability and sustaining life and culture of living beings, including human beings, on the earth demands a stipulation between man and nature, which leads them for accepting tribal world view toward environmental and ecological attachment. Ecology which fulfills our all requirement and assures lives of flora and fauna, which are also part of it, are in danger in the name of development up to the twenty first century of scientific age. There have been a large number of government and non-government bodies possessing with their many constitute parts throughout the world have been doing many project works for subduing burning ecological issues e.g, climate change, global warming, ozone layer, pollution, bio-diversity and biospheres conservation etc. They have also been trying to make awareness among the people for saving ecology and nature by making an urge for planting, saving water, reducing pollution and waste etc. In spite of all these works "ecology has been facing serious threats" that causes rapid climatic and environmental changes, which has been affecting directly and indirectly on lives of people, and on their economic modes for earning livelihood (Sharma, 2016, p. 1).

Ongoing increasing demands of materialistic world's basis requirements to live a comfortable life like metropolitan cities along with its neighbouring areas, towns and villages, have been forced unwillingly or willingly the people to accommodate with the fast pace of modernisation. All these things and their processes have been comprised with industrialisation and have been giving opportunities to those capitalists and "the intellectual dominance of economics" who want to absorb natural resources from the earth by neglecting the environment and ecological variables in developing planning (Guha, 2011, p. 2). Increasing empire of industrialisation and mining have been caused depleting natural resources by years, e.g., minerals from below the surface and forest-clad from the surface of the Earth.

The processes of industrialisation and mining are directly connected with the disruption of environment, ecology and climate change. Decreasing and increasing the quantity of Oxygen and Carbon dioxide and other greenhouse gases respectively "capture heat from the Sun's energy that radiates from the Earth's surface", known as "greenhouse effect" cause rising temperature, and climate change (Center, 2021, p. 11). Depleting ozone layer has also been the main cause for climate change and for increasing rate of greenhouse effects.

Ecology and Society

The mystery of the evolution of a man is linked with the development of ecological system of the earth. Ecology demonstrates symbiotic "relationships between organisms and their environment" and the "interaction of organisms with each other". The surroundings of the man including all things, organic and inorganic matters, is usually termed as 'environment' and the environment is "etymologically means surroundings". (Kumar & Mina, 2018, pp. 1, 3). Pondering on the above reviews, facets of different terms regarding society, cultural, religious and philosophical thought come across before us as an evolution. Thus, society is the constitute part of the environment and ecology which has been gradually developed by the man's efforts to live in a group for making sustaining and sustainability of his existence and identity. In the processes of making societal structures and its organisations, the man consolidated to environmental and ecological thought for conserving nature and their traditional surrounding.

Ecology is nothing but surrounding of our abode where we live and grow. It comprises interdisciplinary relationship between "population, sentient (flora and fauna), non-sentient (river, woods, rocks etc.) and culture". In 1866, German biologist Ernst Haeckel coined first time a term 'ecology' for connoting it as a science which deals with study of the relationships between "living organisms to the external world, their habitat, custom, energies, parasites etc." (Sharma, 2016, p. 11). By studying advanced researches in anthropology and the records of excavations of archeological history reveal that our existence was made possible going through the accommodated environmental and ecological structure, which gave us the opportunity to exist here. Stepping a head gradually, "we humans came to possess knowledge of things that gave us certain superiority over other organism and consequence our relationship with nature was historically one of dominance" (Caldas, 1998, p. 216). All these things happen in ecology by aeon ago, where we had developed our societal and cultural organisations and their custom and culture in way of our existence on the earth, which gave us religiously and philosophically attachments to the nature and our all modes of earnings also depend on it.

The study of Charles J. Krebs discloses that "the roots of ecology lie in natural history, which is as old as humans. Primitive tribes, which depended on hunting, fishing and food gathering, needed detailed knowledge of where and when their quarry might be found. The establishment of agriculture increased the need to learn about the practical ecology of plant and domestic animals" (1994, p. 4). Pondering on the above review the mystery of evolution of human races, society and culture along with different modes of earning livelihood and economic mode are hidden in the complex and puzzled term "ecology". By study of ecology in context of tribal and indigenous peoples could be understood better for providing a solution for climate resilience of climate change.

Ramachandra Guha ponders on "the realm of 'high' culture" which "brings us to the environment debate proper — i.e., the study of the attitudes of different religious and political philosophies to nature, and the emergence of the new theories of environment and development" (2011, p. 7). Further he analysed many scholars e.g., Orlove (1980)[1], Weiskel (1983)[2], and Brokensha (1987)[3] in the context of environment and revealed that "anthropology has deplored the neglect of indigenous resource management institutions in developing planning, and has stressed the importance of local control and knowledge in ensuring sustainable use of the environment" (Guha, 2011, p. 8). Analysing on the above review, the society and culture is associated with environment and ecology where man has gradually acquired knowledge and technically become advanced today.

Climate Change

Rapid growth of world population forces us to adapt economic mode of mass production for supplying all the materialistic requirements sustainability for food, shelter, cloth, ornament, and also tools and equipment for establishing numerous industries. All these things have been fulfilled by converting natural resources into commodities in the forms of marketable products which have been going on by hundreds of years. With the growing empire of industrialisation and mining have been making threats of climate change on the existence of living beings which arise a burning question in our contemporary timeline before us where life will be sustained on the earth or not. A study by Shweta Jayawardhan discloses that due to exhausting emissions of pollution particles, wastes and greenhouse gases etc. cause "anthropogenic climate change is adversely affecting the Earth's environment and altering the ways in which people live" (Jayawardhan, 2017, p. 104).

Climate change is scientifically not a new term but going on from aeon ago. Its early phases involved the evolution in developing and growing our planet as a green planet; and later which caused to the series of evolution

[1] Orlove, B., (1980). Ecological Anthropology, *Annual Review of Anthropology*, Vol. 9 pp. 235-73

[2] Weiskel, T.C., (1983). Rubbish and Racism: Problem of Boundary in an Ecosystem, *Yale Review*, Winter, pp. 225-44

[3] Brokensh, D.W., (1987). Development Anthropology and Natural Resource Management, *L'Uomo: Societal Tradizine Sviluppo*, Vol. 11, No. 2, pp. 225-47

of growing organism into homo sapiens to modern man; but nowadays it became threats on our existence by exhaustive absorbing and exploitation natural resources. In 1988, Intergovernmental Panel on Climate Change (IPCC) was established for "consensus on and fostering an international forum for assessing the science of climate change" whose duty is to "regular assessment on the state of climate knowledge, forecasts future changes, and offers emission reduction policy recommendations to the Unites Nation." The findings of the panel indicate that what happened if the global warming raised by two degrees Celsius above, there will happen a series of "plethora of disastrous environmental consequences. Sea levels would rise by a meter or more, swallowing up coastal and low-lying swaths of the planet's remaining forests. Some regions would experience heavy rain and flooding, while others would suffer protracted period of severe drought. Extreme weather events, such as tornados and hurricanes, would become more common." (Park, 2015, p. 190).

Altering climate change has been directly proportional, and effected hazardously to the following categories: agriculture, forestry, weather and environment, sea levels rise, health issues and many other things related to ecology. When the processes of climate change reaches high level, each and everything of our ecosystem will be endangered to be remaining in their existence in the original forms. As per the study by Richard S.J. Tol (2011) and Cheryl Cox Macpherson (2014) reveals that "people can die prematurely due to climate change, or they can migrate because of sea level rise" or would be forced to live in hunger, scarcity and poverty in deserted lives because there would be nothing, but monsoon means drought, flood or excessive rain etc. (Tol, 2011, pp. 3, 5; Macpherson, 2014).

Ecological Tribal World View

The vast and rich knowledge systems of nature 'ecology' of the tribes as well as indigenous peoples, which have been developed in the way of their living from aeon ago where they inhabited or migrated to from and later settled on a specific geographical location. Further growing healthier spiritual and religious relationship with the nature and surroundings provided them basic requirement for existence and sustainability e.g., food, shelter, and security etc. Over centuries, they have mainly earned livelihood from those of ecological and geographical natural resources and there constructed their own societal structural organisations and their norms centralising to nature 'ecology' such as custom and culture, views and values regarding environmental and ecological philosophy for sustainability. Nowadays advance researches in different disciplines of social science e.g. anthropology, history, sociology, and social work etc. recognised the relevance of the tribal worldviews in the context of their society, custom, culture, philosophy etc. Some of them are generally recognised as "traditional resources", "traditional knowledge system" and "ecological tribal worldview" in the context of man, nature and 'ecology'.

Most of the tribal and indigenous peoples of different parts of the world earn their livelihood by traditional resources located in surroundings, nearby their settlements and villages, where they have been inhabited for years. The traditional resources comprise the village land and other arable lands locating in woods, slop of hills and riverine sides, where they practise different modes of agriculture e.g. slash and burn 'swidden agriculture' along with settled agriculture; undulating terrain for agricultural purpose which is the hallmark of practising science and technology in making and tilling them arable lands; forests for foraging and hunting, and collecting fruit, root, stem, leave and herbal medicinal things etc.; fountain sleeps, springs, hill wells are used as embankments for conserving drinking water source, bathing and other community based requirement etc. what have mentioned above demonstrate environment and ecological attachment of tribal and indigenous peoples for sustainability in their habitats.

Life and lives of tribal and indigenous peoples of Jharkhand along with different parts of India and world primarily depend on the nature and traditional resources, are very intricate pattern. From the beginning of the mid of sixteen century to twenty first century up to the present, those regions have been opened for outer world different culture and custom from them and gradually introduced with many development programmes of industrialisation such as mining industries, reservoir projects, power plants and many other factories with rigorous rules and regulations which have been resulting exhaustive abuses of exploitations in the name of economic development of the country as well as the tribal and indigenous peoples.

These all along with economic development programmes had adversely affected them, and environment and ecology whose consequences have been mentioned above that have been resulted into crisis among the tribal and indigenous peoples of India along different parts of the world. To optimise such crisis, various interventional development programmes have also been introduced at national and international levels by different organisations of governmental and non-governmental body, but tribal peoples show their resistance and antagonism as soon as possible when these all things occur in their geographical and ecological settings.

Analysing on the above matters and reviews, the researcher has found that there is a decisive line between tribal and ingenious people and non-tribal people of different culture from them. Former group of people want to live isolated from different culture of people without any transverse and interventional interruption, and want to enjoy in their own traditional settlement along with their custom and culture which is strongly attached with ecological system. Latter group of people possess different aims and objectives from the former group. Latter group is comprised with non-tribal e.g. the Hindu, Muslim and Christian who want to run missionaries' programmes in the tribal areas for assimilating them in their own community. Actually, they are the big supporter of huge corporate groups and those processes of industrialisation which give them opportunity as missionaries to visit in remote areas where tribal and indigenous peoples are inhabited to soothe their crisis and predicament which make their work easy to assimilate them in their own culture and religion. The dissimilarity which makes tribal and indigenous peoples special is the intrigue attachments to the nature are their religious and philosophical thought towards ecological worldview. Tribal, one who wants to live in their own geographically location e.g. forest-clad rugged and undulating areas, on the slop of the hills, riverine and in the valley has always been involved in opposing the processes of industrialisation and mining in their surroundings.

What happens when corporate groups intrude into those areas the result is they weave concrete like as spider's web for expanding empire of industries and mining. These all cause primarily two burning issues e.g. one is land alienation from tribal and indigenous peoples' traditional resources, 'land

and forest', which snatched the bowl of earning livelihoods from them, and forcing them to live in poverty and scarcity and second is deforestation, which cause one of the terrible global issues in the form of 'climate change' as above mentioned in detail. As a result, in those concurrences as above mentioned, there has been happened a series of environmental and ecological movements in those areas where tribal and indigenous peoples inhabited possess glorious history but unfortunately most of them have not come before us in detailed and written context. Some of environmental and ecological movements of State Jharkhand in Eastern India are Koel Karo People's Movement, Khunti and its adjacent districts in Jharkhand, Eastern India (1970s-2010); Ban Bachao Andolan, Kolhan Regions, Chaibasa in Jharkhand, Eastern India (1980s); Resistance against Netarhat Field Firing Range, districts of Latehar, Lohardaga and Gumla in Jharkhand, Eastern India (1994–till date); Pathalgadi Movement, Khunti and its adjacent districts in Jharkhand, Eastern India (2014-2019/20).

Here are also being disclosed some other environmental and ecological movements in the developing countries e.g. "Chipko Andolan (Hug the Tree Movement), Garhwal in Uttarakhand, North India (1973–mid 1980s); Silent Valley Movement, Palakkad in Kerala, South India (1976-83); Narmada Bachao Andolan (Save Narmada Movement) in Madhya Pradesh, Central India (1987-till date); Anti-Chico Dam Movement in Luzon, the Philippines (1972-86); Sarawak Movement, East Malaysia (1980s-1990s); and, Amazonia Rubber Tappers' Movement, Acre, Brazil (mid-1970s-1980s)" (Sharma, 2016) which are totally different from those environmental and ecological movements, which have occurred in those areas of tribal and indigenous peoples. Former is fought for sustainability of their existence, indenting and conserving their societal and cultural norm, custom and value; and latter is fought for conserving nature and ecology which is found in former also.

Conclusion

Based on the above researches and reviews, the result reveals that, in the context of tribal ecological worldview, these all environment and ecological movements not only demonstrate collective actions, but also reveal the hallmark of religious and ecological worldview for conserving natural resources as the identities of their existence. Broadly speaking, these movements urge to ponder over protection and recognition their traditional rights over natural resources 'Jal, Jungle and Jamin' as their cultural legacy, which has been bestowed them through one generation to another; and also, our constitution provides them constitutional rights over natural resources, which are located in fifth and sixth schedules. There are constitutional provisions as safeguard the right of tribal and indigenous people to preserve their culture, protection of environment and maintenance of ecological balance which is the prime concerns of the government but failed. Analysing and observing climatic issues, the researcher has delineated that the societal and cultural activities of tribal people have been closely associated with their ecological perspective and all these are present in ecological tribal worldview. These movements throw light not only on enlarged vision of economic and politics concerns, but also worldwide burning issues of climate change as a solution for climate resilience.

Suggestions

- The scientific perspective and tribal ecological worldview behind 'why people protest' for conserving forest-clad and natural resources should be entitled in curriculum of school, college and university as a solution for climate resilience.
- There should be established research institutes for making documentation and archives of these environment and ecological movements; and, for publishing them as output in the form of books.

References

Caldas, A. (1998, July). On Man, Nature, Society, and Ecology: Foreword. *Bulletin of the Ecological Society of America, 79*(3), 216-217.

Center, E.W. (2021). *Global Climate Change: Causes and Indicators.* East-West Center (2021). Online URl: https://www.jstor.org/stable/resrep28811.4.

Guha, R. (Ed.). (2011). *Social Ecology* (3 ed.). New Delhi: Oxford University Press.

Jayawardhan, S. (2017). Vulnerability and Climate Change Induced Human Displacement. *Consilience: The Journal of Sustainable Development, 17*(1), 103-142.

Krebs, C.J. (1994). *Ecology: The Experimental Analysis of Distribution and Abundance* (4 ed.). California: Additional-Wesley Educational Publishers.

Kumar, P., & Mina, U. (2018). *Fundamentantals of Ecology and Environment* (2 ed.). New Delhi: Pathfinder Publication.

Macpherson, C.C. (2014, April). Climate change matters. *Journal of Medical Ethics, 40*(4), 288-290.

Park, J.T. (2015). Climate Change and Capitalism. *Consilience: The Journal of Sustainable Development, 14*(2), 189-206.

Sharma, S. (2016). *Why People Protest: An Analysis of Ecological Movement* (2nd ed.). New Delhi: Publications Division.

Tol, R.S. (2011). *Climate Change: The Economic Impact of Climate Change in the 20th and 21th Centuries.* Copenhagen Consensus Center. Online URL: http://www.jstor.com/stable/resrep16376

9

Mainstreaming Child Centric Disaster Risk Reduction in Panchayati Raj Institutions

Balu I

Introduction

Panchayat institutions are our heritage. In India, the village level governance by the native people through *Panchayats* has the history of more than 2000 years. From Vedic period of Sabha-Samithy system of village governance (in the Chola's Kingdom), it has great significance in village administration (Aslam, 2007). Feature of these institutions were largely self-governing by the social structure. Between ancient, medieval and modern periods, the growth of Panchayats had ups and downs. The Panchayats were introduced in the Indian constitution under Article 40 — the Directive Principles of State Policy, which was just optional and cannot be legally challenged.

Continuous efforts of the civil societies and the political leaders of India, the Indian government took intensive steps to strengthen Panchayat from the late seventies till nineties, the importance of local government institutions was realised by the Indian government. The local self-government was constitutionally approved during 1992 by the 73rd Amendment act. The 73rd constitutional amendment generated great expectations. The local government was considered as of a third stratum of government at the grassroot level. It provided a mandated status in constitution to the Panchayats (The Constitution of India, 1950). As the result of 73rd Amendment, now we have about three million representatives as people leaders in grassroots' institutions.

Salient Features of 73rd Constitutional Amendment

The provision of the act with regard to the states can be broadly categorised as mandatory and discretionary provisions. The mandatory provisions insist the establishment of *Gram Sabha* at village level, establishment of three tier system of Panchayati Raj, direct elections to the Panchayats, reservations for scheduled caste, scheduled tribe and women, constitution of state finance commission and constitution of district planning committee at district level (Alok, 2011). As the subject of Panchayat Raj institutions is under the domain of the state list in the Indian federal system, the central act has therefore given discretionary powers to the state on devolution of powers, functions, authority and finance etc.

Children in Disasters

Children are vulnerable due to their age and dependency on adults for their basic needs such as food, water, hygiene, shelter, care, protection and for their day to day needs and survival. The death rate among the children is higher than adults in the disasters and emergencies situation in South Asia. Children are often vulnerable and it is observed in past three decades in India (Sawai-2012). The children are directly and indirectly affected by disasters by death, injury, dehydration, malnutrition, water and sanitation and the conditions were exacerbated by the climate change (Lawler, 2011). During disasters and emergencies the children's education, and mental health also being affected and they are in psychological trauma. The children were also separated from their family members which increase the vulnerability of children trafficking, exploitation and abuse (Seballos, 2011). The review of literatures are evident that the children are vulnerable and victims to the disasters. As per United Nations Convention on Rights of the Children (UNCRC) the children have rights to participation so it is essential to involve children in disaster risk reduction activities.

Concept of Child Centric Disaster Risk Reduction (CCDRR)

The Child Centric Disaster Risk Reduction (CCDRR) as an emerging concept had a rapid growth and interest among the stakeholders during present decade. CCDRR is linked to the community-based disaster risk reduction and Disaster Risk Reduction for the children with the children. (Plan UK, 2010). The CCDRR is an rights based approach, it emphasis on four principles of the United Nations Convention on Rights of the Children i.e., (i) Non Discrimination, (ii) The best interest of the child, (iii) Right to life, (iv) Views of the children (Plan UK, 2010).

The CCDRR is involving children in DRR and DRR for the children and with the children. It addresses the right holders and duty bearers to safeguard the children's rights during disasters and emergencies. It aims to strengthening the accountability mechanism between rights holders and duty bearers through creating awareness among the right holders about their rights and the duty bearers to realise their roles and responsibilities to protect and fulfil the rights of the children at the times of disasters and emergencies.

Panchayati Raj Institutions and Child Centric Disaster Risk Reduction

Local government institutions, the village Panchayat institution, which is the nearest government institution and has link with local communities have significance in triggering the development at grassroot level. Especially on disaster risk reduction, role of village Panchayats are obligatory. In the incident of disaster caused unforgettable damages to thousands of lives to various states of India, evidenced sharp and immediate reflection for rescue and risk reduction from local Panchayat institutions. Fortunately, these Village Panchayats were not duly recognised and given with preparative perspectives. Many times, panchayats operate with relief mode. Being closer and immediate government system for the local community, it can react intensively beyond relief and restoration activities to preparedness perspectives.

Mainstreaming CCDRR in Panchayati Raj Institutions

The PRIs are gross root organisation which is a legal body and it can play an effective role in Child Centric DRR activities. The Constitution of India, Article 243 G declares the powers, authority and responsibilities of Panchayats. The matters listed in the Eleventh Schedule indicate the responsibility of panchayats in Women and Child welfare. So as per the constitution (Article 243 G) the PRI has primary role in Child welfare. Considering the legal provision for welfare of the children it is essential to mainstream the CCDRR activities in PRIs to ensure the rights of the children during disasters and emergencies.

Activities for Mainstreaming Child Centric DRR

To mainstream the Child Centric DRR at Panchayati Raj Institutions, the following activities were proposed and discussed in detail with legal provision for implementation of the CCDRR activities at PRIs.

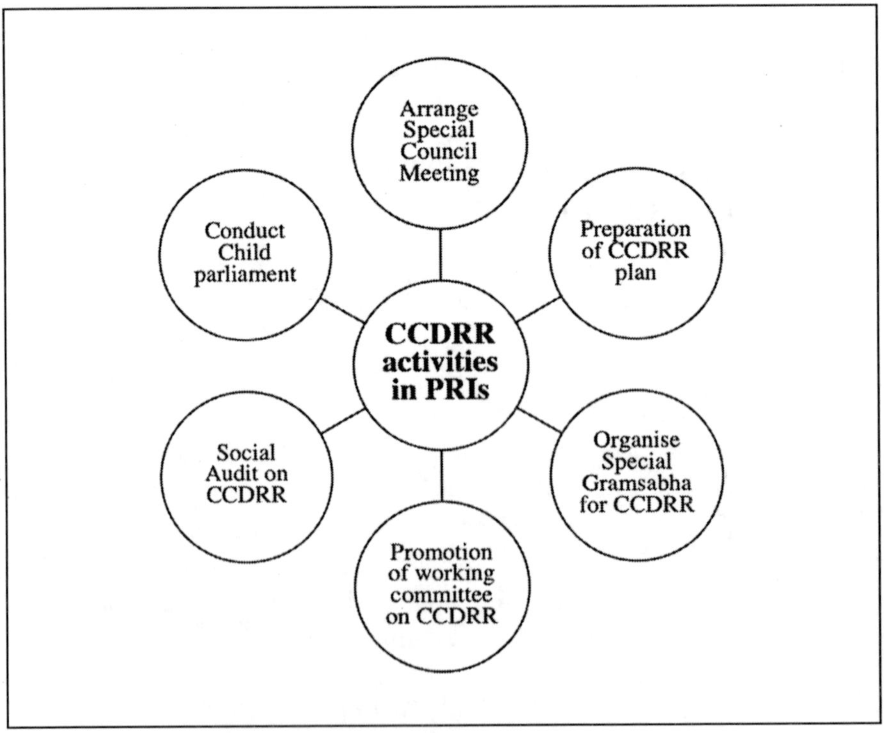

Chart 9.1: Activities for Mainstreaming Child Centric DRR

Conducting Special Panchayat Council Meeting

Conducting panchayat council meeting is a mandatory for all the village panchayats and the panchayats have a provision to conduct a special council meeting to discuss and take resolution on one particular agenda. By using this opportunity all the village panchayats can conduct a special council meeting to discuss on Child Centric DRR issues in their panchayats. The panchayat council members can discuss the child specific issues in their ward and take resolution to address the issues. Basically, the panchayat council can take a resolution to prepare a child centric DRR annual plan for their panchayats. Since, it is a special council meeting for CCDRR so the council should give importance to discuss only CCDRR and they should not discuss any other agenda as per guidelines of council meeting. Jayshree, Mangubhai and S.J. Emma Sydenham (2009) reported that Dalit women's right to political participation in Rural Panchayati Raj. A study of Gujarat and Tamil Nadu was discussed that local councils directly elected by the people are responsible for making decisions on an array of public good decisions.

Preparation of Child Centric DRR Plan

As per Indian constitutional provision Article 243 G, all the village panchayats are mandated to prepare a village development plan and the same can be implemented by the working committees and with the facilitation of panchayat council. Every year all the village panchayats can prepare a Child Centric DRR plan. During the planning process the panchayat should include the children as well as all the stakeholders to prepare an annual development plan with special focus on CCDRR. Debraj Bhattacharya (2019) discussed in his study that the Gram panchayats in Maharashtra initiated Child Friendly Panchayats. It was found that children were actively involved in the affairs of the Gram Panchayat and a child audit was carried out to appreciate the issues related to the development of children. A development plan for the development of the children of the village was prepared in Rajvihir Gram Panchayat in Maharashtra, which was taken up in the pilot phase. In Vandhli Gram Panchayat, possible child-friendly activities were identified. In general, the pilot initiative was successful in the participation of children in

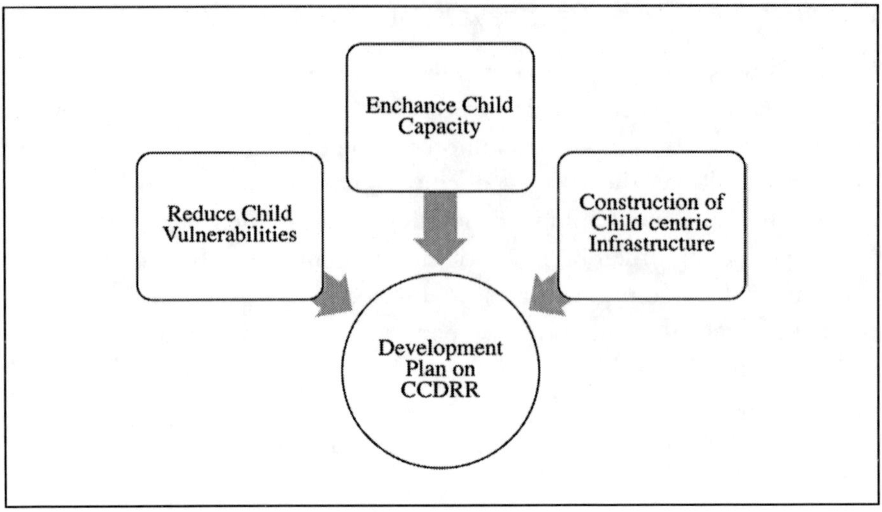

Chart 9.2: Components of Development Plan on CCDRR

their development process, community and Gram Panchayat functionaries were aware of the dimensions of development of children and protecting their rights.

Organising Special Gram Sabha for CCDRR

Indian Constitution Article 243 discuss about the Gram Sabha and its mandates at village panchayat level. Gram Sabha is a legal forum, which discusses and takes resolutions to solve the problems of the village. The panchayats also have powers to organise a special Gram Sabha meeting for discussing specific issues. To mainstream CCDRR at village panchayat level all the village panchayats can organise a special Gram Sabha to discuss the child centric disaster risk reduction activities and approval of CCDRR plan prepared at panchayat level (Mahipal, 2009), discussed in their study that the Gram sabha plays a vital role in decision-making and encourages people participation for their welfare.

Promotion of Child Centric DRR Working Committees

Village panchayats in India were mandated to form different working committees. It also varies from state to state. In Tamil Nadu it is called

Working Committees *(Tamil Nadu Panchayat Raj Act Section -101)* and in Kerala, it is called Standing Committees similarly each state has their own name and committees according to their state Panchayat Raj Act. The panchayats were formed five to seven working committees and it varies from state to state with reference to State Panchayati Raj Act. To reduce the disaster risk reduction of children, all the village panchayats can promote working committee on Child Centric Disaster Risk Reduction at their panchayat level. Like other committees, the working committee on CCDRR also will be an official forum at panchayat level. The CCDRR working committee should function like other committees in panchayats. The bye laws of other committees can be applicable to the committee on CCDRR also and can make necessary changes wherever required. The Department of Rural Development and Panchayati Raj, Government of Rajasthan, had ordered for constituting the panchayat level child protection committees in all the gram panchayats to ensure the child friendly environment protecting children from the natural disasters as well as man-made disasters.

Social Audit on CCDRR

The panchayats are mandated to conduct a social audit to assess the implementation process of schemes including expenditure, benefits, following the guidelines etc. It is a democratic process which gives a right to beneficiary to assess the process. Social Audit for CCDRR also can be conducted at village panchayat level. Social Audit committee for CCDRR should be promoted with the participation of children and the children should be trained to conduct the Social Audit process. Once in a year the Social Audit for CCDRR should be conducted to assess the schemes implemented for CCDRR which is in CCDRR plan of the panchayats. The Social Audit committee should critically review the schemes and submit the report to panchayat council to rectify the audit queries.

Conducting Child Parliament

Child parliament is a forum, which consists of Children (Beneficiary), Panchayat council (Implementing Agency) and speaker who facilitates the parliament process. Once in a year it can be organised and discuss the children's issues and the implementation of annual plan of CCDRR. Child parliament is a well-established concept which can be organised at all the village panchayats. The active participation of children is essential in child parliament. The child parliament will give an opportunity for the children to participate in development process and seeking for their rights. Though all the panchayats were not experienced in this, so the village panchayat can seek the support of civil society organisation for implementation of the Children parliament at their village panchayat level. Once the panchayats gained the experience further the panchayat can do themselves without depending on others. Gandhi Mary Arun Kumar (2014) mentioned in their study that the children parliament had an impact on leadership skills, health and education of children.

Process of Mainstreaming CCDRR Activities

Though all the activities discussed were different but it has linkage between each activity. The panchayats can implement each activity alone based on the needs of the panchayats or it is better to implement the CCDRR activities step by step explained below. The first year it can be done sequentially but later all the forums will function regularly focusing their responsibility.

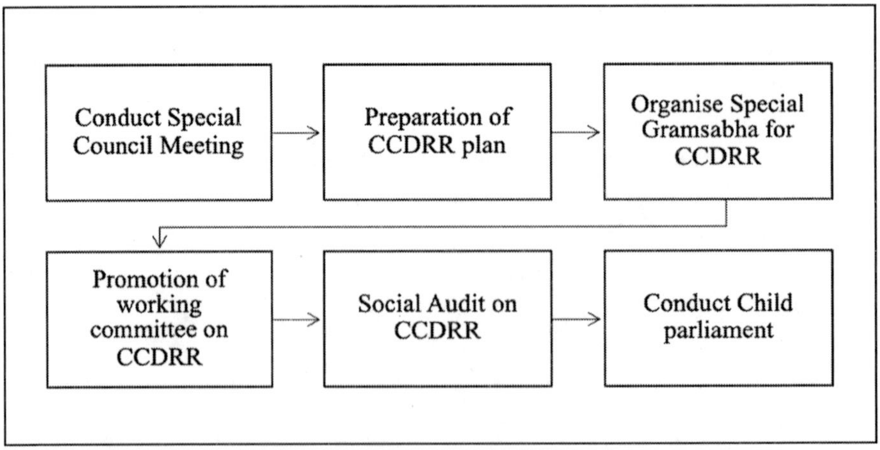

Chart 9.3: Process of mainstreaming CCDRR activities

Strategies for Mainstreaming CCDRR in PRIs

- Mainstreaming CCDRR in PRIs requires creating the capacity building of village panchayat presidents. Once the presidents were aware of the importance of CCDRR then the panchayats themselves will start implementing the CCDRR activities in their panchayats and it will be simple to approach the stakeholders.
- As a part of Sansad Adarsh Yojana, Member of Parliament can take this is an opportunity and implement the thematic model village by implementing CCDRR activities. This thematic Adarsh Gram should be showcased for learning of others. The Member of Parliament has enough funds for implementation so there is no financial issue also to implement the CCDRR at panchayat level.
- UNICEF works in over 190 countries and territories to save children's lives, to defend their rights, and to help them fulfill their potential, from early childhood through adolescence. It also presents in India and implementing Child centric DRR activities. So UNICEF can explore this to implement at village panchayat level partnering with local government. In addition to that the international humanitarian organisations like Save the Children, Child Rights and You, World vision also can implement CCDRR activities through village panchayats.
- The state government, which is willing to implement the Child Friendly Panchayats (CFP) activities also can implement the CCDRR activities.
- The Government of India can also offer Subhash Chandra Bose Aapda Prabandhan Puraskar award to the Panchayati Raj Institutions for their excellent work in Disaster Management, which will motivate the Panchayati Raj Institutions to Mainstream CCDRR activities.
- The Department of Women and Child Welfare, National Commission on Protection of Child Rights (NCPCR) also allocates fund to the village panchayats to implement CCDRR activities at gross root level.
- Since the CCDRR is an emerging concept and at the same time it is important to implement CCDRR at the field level to protect the children from emergencies. The children are the future pillar of our country so it is essential that all the stakeholders: Union Government,

State Government, Local Government, People, Children and Civil society organisation needs to work together to protect the children from disasters impact.

Way Forward

Child Centric DRR is a new concept and essentially needs priority. Union government and State governments were realising the importance and initiated few activities like School safety and mock drill to the children but it is important to work in all aspects of CCDRR. The stakeholders should make bottom-up approach to mainstream CCDRR in Panchayati Raj Institutions for the betterment of the children.

References

1. Ajinder Walia & Sushma Guleria. (2012). Village Disaster Management Plan. National Institute of Disaster Management, New Delhi - 110002, Pages 103. https://www.india.gov.in/spotlight/saansad-adarsh-gram-yojana
2. Alok, V.N. (2011). Role of panchayat bodies in rural development since 1959. Paper presented at the Fifty-Fifth Members Annual Conference. New Delhi: Indian Institute of Public Administration.
3. Aslam, M. (2007). Panchayati Raj in India, New Delhi: National Book Trust, India.
4. Debraj Bhattacharya. (2019). Gram Panchayat Development Plans in Maharashtra, India: An Analysis, Technical Report, Research Gate.
5. Gandhi, Mary & Arun Kumar. (2014). Role of Children Parliament in Tiruvannamalai District – A Descriptive Study, *Indian Journal of Applied Research*, 4(12).
6. Jayshree Mangubhai. (2009). *Obstacles to the Effective Political Participation of Dalit Women*, Geneva, p.1. Retrieved from www.ohchr.org.
7. Lawler, J. (2011). *Children's Vulnerability to Climate Change and Disaster Impacts in East Asia and the Pacific*. uniCeF eaPro, Bangkok. available at: www.unicef.org/media/media_60507.html
8. Mahipal. (2009). *Gram Sabha Meetings in India: Processes, Outcomes and Perspectives*, JOAAG, Vol. 4. No. 2, p.85. Retrieved from joaag.com.
9. Ms. Krupa, V.D. (2016). Role of Social Audit in development of rural area through PRIs – A case study of Shimoga region, *ISBR Management Journal*, 1(2), 84-85.

10. Patricio Cuevas-Parra. (2015). Children's parliament and children's council in World vision programme, World vision Bangladesh.
11. Plan UK.(2010). *Child-centred Disaster Risk Reduction: Building Resilience through Participation – Lessons from Plan International.* Plan UK, London. available at: https://plan-international.org/about-plan/resources/publications/emergencies/child-centred-disaster-risk-reduction-building-resilience-through-participation/
12. Rural Development and Panchayat Raj Department, Government of Rajasthan, Child friendly Panchayat initiative, Hand Book
13. Sawai, M. (2012). *Who is Vulnerable During Tsunamis? Experiences from the Great East Japan Earthquake 2011 and the Indian Ocean Tsunami 2004.* unescap, Bangkok. available at: www. unescap.org/sites/default/files/idd-drs-who-is-vulnerable-during-tsunamis.pdf
14. Seballos, Fran, Tanner T., Tarazona, M. & Gallegos, J. (2011). *Children and Disasters: Understanding Impact and Enabling Agency.* Children in a Changing Climate, Institute of Development Studies, Brighton. available at: www.ids.ac.uk/publication/children-and-disasters-understanding-impact-and-enabling-agency
15. The Constitution of India 1950, Art 243.

10

Environmental Ethics and Teacher Competencies

High School Teachers' Attitude towards Teaching Biodiversity

V. Mercy Jyothi and P. Renuka

Environmental Ethics Education

Ethics belongs to the field of values. Environmental ethics includes, "Principles and Values that a man as an individual and as a member of the society should follow so as to Conserve, Preserve and Manage the Environment" as mentioned by Saxena in 2003. Thus, ethics has a direct association with human behaviour through the value system developed by an individual in the society. However environmental values raise certain questions as "what is environmentally good?" and "what is bad?". Environmental ethics relates to doing, "what is good" and "not doing what is bad". Environmental ethics deals with the ethical relationship between human beings and the environment, where humans are a part. Thus, Environmental ethics aims to analyse and develop, how an individual must behave or what rules and moral obligations an individual must have while interacting with his environment. These moral commitments reflect the set of standards for decision-making, picking out alternatives and actions.

Biodiversity as Theme in Environmental Education at Secondary School Level

Environmental Education comprises of specific issue-oriented topics and one of such topics is Biodiversity education. There is a growing trend to divide environmental education into particular issues as said earlier. Obviously, there would be great disadvantage in forming more groups of separate disciplines as each individual discipline creates and constructs its own facts, concepts, theories and principles, which comes under substantive structure of science, and non-availability of space in the curriculum framework. But infusing these as themes instead of separate disciplines, of Environmental Education helps productively with much more consistency in reaching the purposeful educational objectives. Environmental Education provides an interdisciplinary format for making citizens of the globe to cope up with problems and issues relating to biodiversity.

Psychological aspect is also a reason for the trend of breaking environmental education into simpler themes as environmental problems are complex and massive and solving this task requires greater intellectual ability.

Environmental education consists of biodiversity as one of the major components. The Supreme Court of India issued an order to the Government of India to infuse Environmental Education in the school curriculum. The result of this is, science textbooks for primary classes are entitled as 'Environmental Sciences' and at high school level, Biodiversity has been infused as separate units after the recommendations of "*XI Convention on Biodiversity*". So, the ultimate target is the youth of high school classrooms must in turn cope up with the causes, solutions and consequences of Biodiversity issues. However, the immediate target audiences are the "*Teachers — who deal with Biodiversity*".

Competencies of a Science Teacher to Teach Biodiversity Component

Definition given by De Ketele in 1996 says, "A competence is a set of organised capacities, which act on contents in a given category of situations in order to solve a problem." In this definition, competence is described as an ability to carry out a specified task or activity to predetermined standards of attainment. De Bueger Van der Borght C. in 1996, says, "Competence refers to a state of being well qualified to perform an activity or a task. When a person is competent to do something, he or she has achieved a state of competence that is recognisable and verifiable to a particular community of practitioners. A competency, then, refers to the way that a state of competence can be demonstrated to the relevant community."

To be competent in a certain area implies the ability to mobilise one's own knowledge and to transform into concrete doing. Competency is an individual's characteristic and is built through self-experiences and formation in a given area of problems as mentioned by Adrienne Kozan in 2008.

UNESCO-United Nations Environment Programme (UNEP), Environmental Education Series 25, "Strategies for the Training of Teachers in Environmental Education", in its document emphasised on various strategies of Environmental Education programmes. The Environmental Education programme emphasises at various grade levels, should differ according to the needs and capabilities of the receivers. Therefore, it may be expected that teachers at all levels and in various disciplines, may require more or less competency to deal with the area of Environmental Education. A high school teacher for example, may require more expertise in the use of case studies as investigative models than it is required by a Primary Level Teacher. However, the need for some degree of competency in each of the following areas will remain for all effective environmental education teachers.

Classification of Competencies in Environmental Education

Competencies in Environmental Education content have been classified into IV levels according to UNESCO-UNEP Environmental Education Series 25. They are as follows

Level I: Ecological Foundations
Level II: Conceptual Awareness
Level III: Investigations and Evaluations
Level IV: Environmental Action Skills

Directions Given by the Supreme Court on Environmental Education

The aspect of Environmental Education has been very rightly upheld by the Supreme Court in the case of Sri. M.C. Mehta. In 1991, Sri M.C. Mehta filed an application in the public interest (writ petition, civil) No. 860 of 1991, asking the supreme court to:

1. Issue directions to cinema hall that they show slides with information on the environment.
2. Issue directions for the spread of information relating to the environment on All India Radio.
3. Issue directions that the study of environment becomes a compulsory subject in schools and colleges.

On 18th December 2003, the Honourable Supreme Court, ordered the NCERT to develop and design a model syllabus. On 13th July 2004, the Supreme Court directed that "the syllabus designed by the NCERT for Class I to XII shall be adopted by every state in their respective schools". It further directed that NCERT should be appointed as a nodal agency to supervise the implementation of the Supreme Court's order. NCERT developed the syllabus for environmental education from Class I to XII standards which was accepted by Supreme Court as in the Document on 13th July 2004. But this syllabus has been subsequently reviewed and revised in the light of National Curriculum Framework (NCF) 2005.

The current method of implementation of Environmental Education in schools is as follows according to NCERT's Affidavit to Supreme Court.

Classes	Mode of Transaction
I-II	Through activities
III-V	Environmental studies (EVS)
VI-X	Infusion Model

So, at high school level, Environmental Education is transacted through infusion model in all school disciplines, i.e., Biological Sciences, Physical Sciences, Mathematics, Social sciences along with Languages. When compared to the content of Environmental Education in all the above-mentioned disciplines, it is found that Biological Sciences Textbooks cover majority of the topics related to environmental sciences. The environmental science topics that are covered in High School Biological Science textbooks are "Our surroundings", "Environment", "Biotic and Abiotic components", "Classification of Ecosystems", "Natural resources (Renewable and Non-renewable resources)", "Types of pollutions" and "Biodiversity". Biodiversity is an important aspect that is to be emphasised in the present situation especially in our country where, India is one of the Mega Biodiversity countries with 7 per cent of all globally recorded species. The XI conference of the parties, "the convention on biological diversity" was held in India during 1-19 October 2012 at Hyderabad, the then capital of united Andhra Pradesh. Basing on the reports of the convention, Biodiversity has been given due importance and it has been included in the high School Biological Science curriculum along with other themes of Environmental sciences.

Significance

Environment means surroundings, in which organisms survive. It refers to both Biotic and Abiotic components of Earth. Existence of life on earth is impossible without environment. On the other hand, human beings are over-exploiting the natural resources available at an alarming rate, without any discrimination leading to destruction and deterioration of the environment.

So, the protection of environment with sustainable development is necessary and need of the hour. In the way of environmental protection, environmentally ethical attitude plays a key role and values of environmental ethics can be achieved mainly through education. Consequently, the schools have to take a lead role in developing right type of future society wherein each member is socially as well as environmentally responsible and is to be competent for Environment Oriented Action.

Environmental ethics, human attitudes, values that influence individual behaviour and government policies towards nature capable of governing human actions will affect the nature as was stated by Callicott, 1995 and Jardins, 2001. So Environmental Ethics of every individual influences his behaviour and this is applied even to teachers most importantly. From this, specifically, it can be said that the attitude of Environmental ethics of a teacher influences their behaviour. When it comes to Biological Science Teachers, environmental ethics influences their behaviour, which covers most of the environment-oriented themes. As teaching becomes a part of their behaviour, it indeed means that Biological Science teacher, while teaching biodiversity component, reflects their ethical behaviour towards environment with quality in teaching.

When it comes to teaching, a qualitative and effective teacher is usually assessed by his competencies. "Of all the different factors, which influence the quality of education and its contribution to National Development, the equality, competence and characters of teachers are undoubtedly the most significant according to Indian Education Commission 1964-66. So, from the words of Dr. Daulat Singh Kothari, the factors those influence quality also contribute to *competence,* which is to be considered significantly".

Therefore, it becomes necessary to assess the relationship between environmental ethics of a teacher and his competencies to Teach Environmental Education Component. In this present context it specifically implies a study on the Attitude towards Environmental Ethics and their Competencies in Teaching Biodiversity Component of High School Biological Sciences Teachers.

The Study

Objective

1. To find out the relationship if any, between the Attitude of High School Biological Sciences Teachers towards Environmental Ethics and their competencies in Teaching Biodiversity Component.

Hypothesis There would be no significant difference in the relationship between the Attitude of Secondary School Biological Science Teachers towards Environmental Ethics and their Competencies in dealing with Biodiversity Component.

Method Employed

Descriptive research which is qualitative and also uses non-quantitative methods to describe "what is" as stated by J.W. Best & J.V. Kahn. The present study also describes, records, analyses using suitable statistics and interprets the data. Therefore, in the present study descriptive type of research (survey) is employed by the investigator.

Tools

The following tools are used:

- Environmental Ethics Attitude Scale (EEAS) – Developed by the investigator

The tool is entitled, "*Environmental Ethics Attitude Scale*" (EEAS) consists of 35-statements covering four dimensions of Attitudes, namely,

1. Anthropocentrism (EEA1)
2. Biocentrism (EEA2)
3. Ecocentrism (EEA3)
4. Values (EEA4).

Reliability and Validity of the EEAS

The reliability of EEAS was found to be 0.98. The intrinsic validity of the scale is 0.989 and 0.9949.

- *Biodiversity Competencies Scale (BCS) - Developed by the investigator*

The tool is entitled, "Biodiversity Competencies Scale" (BCS) consists of 36-Statements covering Four dimensions of Competencies are as follows:

1. Level 1: Ecological Foundations (BC1)
2. Level II: Conceptual Awareness (BC2)
3. Level III. Investigations and Evaluations (BC3)
4. Level IV: Environmental Action Skills (BC4)

To check the competencies of Secondary School Biological Science Teachers, in Teaching Biodiversity Component, the investigator analysed the biodiversity content presented in the Secondary School Biological Science textbooks i.e., from VI to X classes, prescribed under Andhra Pradesh state syllabus.

Reliability and Validity of BCS

The reliability of BCS is computed and was found to be 0.79. The Intrinsic Validity of the Scale is 0.891 and 0.940.

Sample

The sample of this study is Secondary School Biological Science Teachers of Chittoor District of Andhra Pradesh, India, with a sample size of 500 teachers. The sampling technique employed was *Purposive Sampling*.

Analysis

To find out the relationship between Attitudes of Biological Science Teachers towards Environmental Ethics and the Competency of teachers in Teaching Biodiversity Component, "Pearson's Product Moment Correlation Coefficient" was computed.

i. Correlation between Attitude of High School Teachers towards Environmental Ethics and their Competencies in Teaching Biodiversity Component

The objective of the present investigation is to find out the relationship between Teachers' Attitude towards Environmental Ethics and their competencies in Teaching Biodiversity Component.

Hypothesis is tested using Pearson's Correlation 'r' and the results are shown in Table-10.1.

Table 10.1: The Correlation of Biological Science Teachers' Attitude towards Environmental Ethics and their Competencies of Biological Sciences Teachers in Teaching Biodiversity Component along with its Dimensions

S. No.	*Competencies of Biological Science Teachers*	*Mean*	*S.D*	*r-Value*	*Level of Significance*
1	EEA1	60.06	13.48	0.098	*
2	EEA2	66.44	13.46	0.044	@
3	EEA3	59.89	16.03	0.089	*
4	EEA4	51.01	14.45	0.131	**
Over all Teachers Attitude		60.35	11057	0.099	*

Note: @ not significant at 0.05 level, * significant at 0.05 level and ** Significant at 0.01 level.

The above table shows that the calculated 'r'-value is 0.099 and is significant as it is greater than critical r-value i.e., 0.088 at 0.05 level of significance for df=498. Hence the Hypothesis is rejected.

It is also very clear that the dimensions, EEA_1, EEA_3, and overall, Teacher Attitude towards Environmental Ethics are correlated significantly with competencies, as the corresponding 'r'-values are greater than that of the critical r-value at 0.05 level, as such the corresponding hypotheses are rejected. And EEA_4 is significantly correlated as the calculated 'r'-value is 0.131 and is greater than critical value i.e., 0.115 at 0.01 levels of significance. Hence, it is inferred that Biological Science Teachers Competencies in Teaching Biodiversity Component are associated with their Attitude towards Environmental Ethics.

Conclusion

Biological Science Teachers Competencies in dealing with Biodiversity Component are associated with their attitude towards Environmental Ethics. So, the development of competencies needs cognizance of Environmental Ethics, which thereby develops Attitude towards Environmental Ethics.

In the National Biodiversity Action plan by Government of India, it is mentioned that formal education is to be promoted as a means for biodiversity conservation and also suggested to design and implement awareness programmes and to incorporate modules on conservation and utilisation of biodiversity in professional training at both at foundation (Pre-service) and professional (In-service levels) levels.

It can be developed by including a component of Environmental Ethics in teacher education curriculum in the paper, philosophical foundations of education at both B.Ed. and M.Ed. The investigator framed a Module on Environmental Ethics.

The module covered the following topics viz., History of Environmental Education, Objectives of Environmental Education, Biodiversity, India as a Mega Biodiversity Nation, Concept of Environmental Ethics, Values in the literature of Environmental Ethics, Anthropocentric Theory of Environmental Ethics, Necessity of Environmental Ethics Education, Environmental Ethics and Environmental Educator, How to Teach Environmental Ethics.

This module can be included in M.Ed. curriculum and with slight modifications, it can be even utilised to include in B.Ed curriculum.

References

1. Anjuli Suhane. (2012). Environmental Ethics of In-service Teachers, Pre-service Teachers and Teacher Educators, RGC *Research Journal.org*, 1(1).
2. A.K.Rai & R.N. Sarma. (2017). Environmental ethics education: A necessity to initiate environment oriented action, *SPIJE*, 7(I).
3. Florica Morar Andrea Peterlicean. (2012). The Role and Importance of Educating Youth Regarding Biodiversity Conservation in Protected Natural Areas, *Elsevier, Science Direct* 3 (2012), 1117 – 1121.
4. Hairul Nizam Ismail, Suhail Mahmoud Al-Zoubi, Majdoleen et al. (2009). Competency Based Teacher Education (CBTE): A Training Module for Improving Knowledge Competencies for Resource Room Teachers in Jordan, *European Journal of Social Sciences,* 10(2).
5. Sarita Ramsaroop & Hugo van Rooyen.(2013).Exploring educator competence in teaching environmental education in schools in Gauteng, *Africa Education Review* (Journal),10(3).
6. Jeanette Randall Wilson, Martha C. Monroe. (2005). Biodiversity Curriculum that Supports Education Reform, *Applied Environmental Education and Communication*, 4:125–138.
7. Chauhan Loveleen. (2016). Comparative study of environmental ethics among teacher trainees for sustainable development with respect to their level of education and some family related variables, ACADEMICIA: *An International Multidisciplinary Research Journal*
8. M. Muthamizhselvan, & A.C. Lal Kumar. (2017). Environmental ethics of secondary students, *International Journal of Multidisciplinary Research and Development*, 4(9),40-43.
9. Nikhat & Khan, Zebun. (2017). Construction and Validation of Environmental Ethics Attitude Scale. *IRAIJEMS*, 7(3), 9.
10. Navarro-Perez, Moramay & Tidball, Keith. (2012). Challenges of Biodiversity Education: A Review of Education Strategies for Biodiversity Education. *International Electronic Journal of Environmental Education.*
11. Petra Lindemann Matthies. (2009). The integration of biodiversity education in the initial education of primary school teachers: four comparative case studies from Europe. *Journal Environmental Education Research*, 15(1).

11

Awareness towards Disaster Management
Study of Sagar University Students

Rama Verma, Ravi Vanguri and Chittibabu Putcha

Introduction

Disaster means an unwanted event, which can damage our life and property at a great extent. It can happen at anytime and anywhere and all of us can become victim of it. Any kind of disaster creates a disturbance in the smooth functioning of the human life. Today, due to wide technical advancement a large number of disastrous events could be detected by the scientists prior of its happening, still we all are helpless as no one can fully escape from its impact if the events occur in nearby areas of an individual. On the other hand, if technology helps to detect the disaster prior of its happening and sometimes carelessness of handling technology, emerges as a cause of great disasters. For instance, Bhopal Gas Tragedy (1984) was a chemical accident considered as world's worst industrial disaster in the history. And the recent Covid-19 Pandemic has shaken the whole world in a variety of ways. We could learn many lessons from these two incidents impact on our human life. It is also accepted that everyone must understand the nature of the nature-phenomena and also showing responsibility in a respectful manner to get things to surviving and protect nature as well. India is such a large developing country with regard to modernisation, infrastructure, technology, education, etc. It is also termed as the land of diversity with great geographical features, which makes India as an incredible country. India was ranked 77th on the World Risk Index (World Risk Report, 2016).

India is categorised into five sub-divisions on the bases of possibility of occurrence of disasters. These are– The Northern Mountain Region, The Indo-Gangetic Plains, The Deccan Plateau, The Western Desert and The Coastal areas. United Nations defined disaster as a serious disruption of the functioning of a community or society, which involve widespread human, material, economic or environmental impacts that exceed the ability of the affected community or society to cope using its own resources. According to the International Federation of Red Cross & Red Crescent Societies, a disaster occurs when a hazard impacts on vulnerable people. The combination of hazards, vulnerability and inability to reduce the potential negative consequences of risk results in disaster.

Types and Causes of Disaster

The disasters, which happen without human interference or error are called as 'natural disasters' for example — heavy rainfall, storms, floods, etc. whereas the 'man-made disasters' are the disasters, which occur due to the technical failure or carelessness and negligence of human beings, we can say that opposite to natural disaster — it may be intentional and unintentional — such as nuclear disaster, fire disaster, chemical disaster, etc. Historical examples of man-made disasters are London's Killer Fog, Bhopal Gas Tragedy, Maha Kumbh Mela stampede in Allahabad.

The great diversity in geographical features of India is majorly responsible for the occurrence of natural disaster because the major five divisions of India have their own uniqueness and become responsible for different kind of disasters like the northern mountain ranges have a possibility of occurrence of snow storms, avalanches, landslides, cloudbursts, cold waves, heavy rainfall, etc. The Indo-Gangetic Plains are considered as drought prone because of flood, the Deccan Plateau — drought and earthquake. The western desert has a risk of drought and sandstorm. The coastal areas have a risk of cyclones and tidal waves. If disasters have a great history in India and all over the world then it can be realised that we are helpless to prevent the happening of natural disasters, but due to technical advancement we can make people well aware about the disasters that can take place at anytime and anywhere in their locality, which helps in the mitigation process a lot. Nowadays, the technology and social media is playing a vital role for mitigating the influence of disasters by creating awareness among masses towards disaster management and preparedness.

The Disaster Management Act (2005) emphasised that for effective disaster management there should be an institutional and coordination mechanism (DM) at the National, State, District and local levels. As directed by this Act, the Government of India (GoI) created a multi-tiered institutional system consisting of the National Disaster Management Authority (NDMA) regulated by the Prime Minister, the State Disaster Management Authorities (SDMAs) ruled by the respective Chief Ministers and the District Disaster Management Authorities (DDMAs) ruled by the District Collectors and assisted by Chairpersons of the local bodies. These bodies have been set up to assist a paradigm shift from the previously relief-centric methodology to a more practical, all-inclusive and assimilated method of firming disaster preparation, mitigation, and crisis reaction.

The Disaster Management Act (2005) was passed by the Parliament of India on December 23, 2005 and demands for National Disaster Management Authority (NDMA), State Disaster Management Authorities (SDMA) and District Disaster Management Authorities (DDMA). The Disaster-Management Act (2005) embraces the procedures taken by the government for disaster management, the part of local authorities, and destructions and penalties. It also orders the formation of a National Institute of Disaster Management (NIDM). A National Executive Committee (NEC) was set up by the Central Government of India under Disaster Management Act (2005). The National Plan of India was drawn up by the National Executive Committee in consultation with state administrations and expert bodies or organisations. The National Plan includes the measures for shunning and mitigating disasters and their special effects, including mitigation measures in development plans, readiness and capacity building to react to any frightening or hazardous disaster (Disaster Management Act, 2005).

National Policy on Disaster Management, 2009

The National Policy on Disaster Management (NPDM) has been developed after the Disaster Management Act, 2005. The NPDM will provide the roadmap for managing disasters in a whole. It laid emphasis on community participation and Panchayati Raj Institutions in order to bring transparency in all the aspects of disaster management such as legal and financial provisions; avoidance, mitigation and awareness, techno-legal administration; response, relief and re-establishment, recovery, research and development. Major objectives of the NPDM are:

- To support prevention, preparedness and resilience through communication, modernisation and training.
- To boost up mitigation measures with the help of technology, traditional wisdom and ecofriendly environment.
- To bring disaster management into main streaming with progressive development process.
- To certify powerful apparatus for diagnosing, assessment and monitoring of disaster risks.
- To develop modern forecasting and timely warning systems assisted with information technology and support media for generating awareness about disaster management.

National Disaster Management Plan, 2016

The National Disaster Management Plan (NDMP) was set up in 2016. It became the very first national plan in India for disaster management. With this plan our country has united its national plan with the Sendai Framework for Disaster Risk Reduction 2015-2030, to which India is a countersigner. The aim of NDPM is to make India disaster resistant and significantly reduce the loss of lives and assets. The prime focus of the plan is to understand disaster as a whole, improving disaster risk methods, early warning, attentiveness, awareness and Building Back Better (BBB).

Key National-level Decision-Making Bodies for Disaster Management

- Cabinet Committee on Security (CCS)
- National Crises Management Committee (NCMC)
- National Disaster Management Authority (NDMA)
- National Executive Committee (NEC)
- National Disaster Response Force (NDRF)
- National Institute of Disaster Management (NIDM).

International Agencies/Bodies for Disaster Management

- Regional Disaster Prevention Unit (RDPU)
- World Meteorological Organization (WMO)
- Asian Disaster Preparedness Centre (ADPC)
- United Nations Environment Programme (UNEP)
- United Nations International Emergency Network (UNIENET).

Present Prime Minister Shri Narindra Modi also gave key agenda for disaster risk reduction. For this there must be an inclusion of all from very poor households to multi-national corporations to states of the nation. All progressive sectors must take up the principles of disaster risk management. There must be a place of women's participation in disaster risk management. In order to develop the global understanding of nature and disaster risks, we must invest in risk mapping. To enhance the productivity of disaster risk management handworks, we must incorporate technology, local capacity and initiatives in this context. A strong network must be established among universities by promoting the use of social media and mobile technologies to work on disaster related matters. After every disaster one must learn from lesson that emerged from disaster and should incorporate it in future.

The Study

Need and Significance

India, due to its, diversity in terms of physiographic, demographic and climatic settings is regarded as one of the disaster susceptible zones of the world. We all know that our country comes with rank second in terms of population after China. The aim of the different polices, plans, and acts is to sensitise the masses for disaster management, preparedness and resilient, which may help to decrease the losses of life livelihood and property. The Disaster Management Act of 2005 and Disaster Management Policy of 2009 considered disasters can be natural or human-made, can happen at anytime and anywhere (National Disaster Management Plan, 2016). Nowadays the government is trying to introduce the disaster management courses as a part of the curriculum at both at school as well as higher education. Maybe it is not separately taught as a subject, but somehow, we can see the topics related to disaster management in the sciences and social sciences at different levels of education. At post-graduation level, it is offered as an elective course for all the departments, where the students have to opt it as per their interest. The aim to introduce this curriculum is just to sensitise the students by creating awareness among them regarding disaster, management and preparedness, which ultimately helps to mitigate the effect of the disaster. Now the question arises, what do they think about disaster management and its preparedness? And do the students have awareness about disaster management and preparedness? In order to find the answer to such kind of questions the researchers made an attempt to conduct this study.

Research Questions

- Are the Post-Graduate students aware of the disaster and its management policies? Do they have an interest to know about disaster management and also to take part in it?
- What kind of opinion do the Post-Graduate students have regarding disaster management and preparedness?
- How do they perceive the role of an individual in avoiding disaster and also to be prepared?

Objectives

- To know the awareness of Post-Graduate students about disaster management and its Policies?
- To measure the opinion of Post-Graduate students concerning the disaster management and its Preparedness.

Methodology

In the present study, the investigators followed a descriptive survey method. A total of 82 Post-Graduate students, who chose disaster management as an open elective course were taken purposefully as a sample of the study at Dr. Harisingh Gour Viswavidyala, Sagar, Madhya Pradesh. The participants were from different departments, i.e. Anthropology (8), Mathematics (2), Applied Geology (23), Management of Business Accounts (2), Applied Geography (14), Zoology (15), Micro-biology (6), Law (4), Computer Sciences (2), and Adult Education (6). Since, all participants were from the various disciplines, the investigators made an attempt to understand their awareness and opinion regarding the disaster management.

Tools

For accomplishing the articulated objectives, the researchers developed a self-constructed questionnaire and opinionnaire for Post-graduate students. These tools were concentrated and items developed in keeping components such as awareness on policies, interest, opinion and responsibility. Initially the researchers developed the tools and sent to the experts of the concerned field for content validation. After receiving their suggestions in terms of intent, content, and language, it was modified and finalised with a total of 30 items. The Table 11.1 shows the number of participants and their demographic identities.

From the Table 11.1, it is seen that 61 per cent of the post-graduate students who took participation in the study were female while 39 per cent of them belonged to male category. It can be inferred that female students might have much interest in disaster management and its preparedness. Out of 82 participants, the majority of the participants (61%) were found to have a diploma course in disaster management. With regard to their locality, 59 per cent were from urban, 29 per cent rural and 29 per cent semi-urban. Although, they were having diploma courses, the majority (88) was found to be untrained in drilling and mocks.

From the Table 11.2, it can be observed that 90 per cent of the participants were aware of the disasters that happen in their locality. More than half of the participants responded that they were aware of mocks and drills while

Table 11.1: Profile of the Research Participants (N=82)

Specification of the Participants	*Percentage (%)*
Gender	
Male	39
Female	61
Locality	
Rural	29
Urban	59
Semi-Urban	12
Training Oriented	
Trained	12
Untrained	88
Diploma / Course	
Yes	61
No	39

Table 11.2: Awareness of Post-Graduate Students about Disaster Management and its Preparedness

S. No.	*Items*	*Agree %*	*Disagree %*
1.	Awareness of the disasters that happen in my locality	90	10
2.	Awareness of mocks and drills of disaster management	51	49
3.	Understanding of functions of mock drill	37	63
4.	Required training for disaster preparedness	95	5
5.	Conduction of disaster drills at university level	24	76

63 per cent voiced that they were having a lack of understanding the function of mock drill. It is also understood from the table that 95 per cent of the participants responded that they were required to have training for disaster preparedness whereas 5 per cent denied it. The majority of the participants were strongly said that their university did not conduct disaster drills.

It is observed from the Table 11.3, although, the majority of the participants (98%) stated that the disaster management course must be incorporated in the curriculum from school-level to higher education, 56 per cent of them

Table 11.3: Responses of Post-Graduate Students regarding their Interest in Disaster Management

S. No.	*Items*	*Agree %*	*Disagree %*
1.	Disaster management course should be practical	56	44
2.	Disaster management courses should be part of the curriculum in school as well as in higher education	98	2
3.	Reading the policies related to disaster management	73	27
4.	Ever worked for rescue team of disaster management	24	76
5.	I am not much interested in the subject disaster management	20	80

were of the opinion to offer this course in the practical way. It is also noticed that 73 per cent of participants responded that they had read the policies related to disaster management whereas 27 per cent disagreed with it. From the analysis of the data, it inferred that participants were found to have a positive view towards disaster management. Further, it also observed that only 24 per cent of them were found to have participated in a rescue team of disaster management.

From the Table 11.4, it is observed that the majority of the post-graduate students (83%) stated that disasters were likely to be happening in their vicinity. Perhaps, that might be the reason 90 per cent of the students responded that they preferred to know disaster plans in their locality. Seventy-one per cent of them believed in imposing stringent punishment on people who violate the rules of disaster plans.

Table 11.4: Responses of Post-Graduate Students about Disaster Plans

S. No.	*Statements*	*Agree %*	*Neutral %*	*Disagree %*
1.	I prefer to know about disaster plans in my locality	90	10	-
2.	I believe that stringent punishment needs to impose on people, who violate rules of disaster plans.	71	24	5
3.	It is the responsibility of the government only to reduce /minimise the impact of disaster on the society.	34	24	42
4.	I think that disasters are likely to be happening in any area.	83	12	5

Table 11.5: Responses of Post-graduate Students with respect to Disaster Management

S. No	*Items*	*Agree %*	*Neutral %*	*Disagree %*
1.	I think that knowledge of disaster management is not essential for everyone.	10	19	71
2.	I think if people who get awareness about disaster management, they can only reduce the impact of disaster.	73	17	5
3.	I look forward to taking part in drill activities, if government/any agency organise at my locality	95	5	-
4.	I am interested to provide my service voluntarily in the National Disaster Rescue Forces (NDRF) if it requires.	83	5	12
5.	Mitigation is a most crucial act, if done appropriately it can reduce the impact of the next disasters.	90	5	5

Table 11.5 shows the responses of the post-graduate students pertaining to the necessity of gaining knowledge about disaster management. Seventy-one per cent of the participants declared that every individual must have the knowledge of disaster management and also, they believed in people who have awareness they could only reduce the impact of disaster (73%). The majority of them were also looking forward to taking part in drill activities (95%) and also had interest to provide their service voluntarily in NDRF if required (83%). The majority of participants of the study believed in mitigation was a significant act to reduce the impact of immediate disasters.

Major Findings

- The study disclosed that the majority of the post-graduate were found to have an interest in the subject of disaster management course (80%), preferred to know disaster plans (90%), interested to take part in drills and ready to provide services voluntarily (83%).
- The current study revealed that 90 per cent of the participants were found to be aware of the disasters that happen in their vicinity.

- More than half of the participants (51%) responded that they were aware of mocks and drills. But 63 per cent declared that they were having a lack of understanding the function of mock drill.
- Additionally, the study discovered that 95 per cent of the participants stated that they were required to undergo training for disaster preparedness.
- The study divulged that the majority of the participants (98%) opined that the disaster management course should be part of the curriculum from school-level to higher education.
- The study noted that 73 per cent of the sampled participants believed that people who were aware of disaster management, they could only reduce the impact of disaster.

Conclusion

India played its role best in disaster management in terms of preparedness, early warnings, findings, rehabilitation, technological interventions, generating awareness through media assistance, campaigning, plans and polices as per the diversity of the nation. Due to great diversity in physiographic and climatic conditions of the different places demand different strategies to deal with. For example, the disasters occur in coastal areas are totally different from mountainous areas, so the awareness and ways to deal with them are obviously different. The effective disaster management strategies and preparedness will not prove only useful for preventing the lives of people, but also helps affected people to rebuild their livelihood in the best possible manner in a shorter duration of time. The present study revealed that the majority of university students are interested in disaster management though they have opted the course. Although, they were having awareness, but felt the mocks and drills related to disaster should be organised periodically as the awareness alone does not work effectively until and unless it put into practice. The policymakers and administrators must work on to run this course at all the level of education not only in the form of theory, but more focus should be on practical which will prove more useful at the time of need. A strong network also must be established among the universities to work on disaster associated difficulties. Along with this, a separate department of disaster management must be set up in each and every university so that majority of the students may select this course. These departments also should have a close link with National Disaster Rescue Force (NDRF) and the mocks and drills-oriented activities would be conducted with the help of team members of NDRF. In a nutshell, the practical activities must be designed and executed under the guidance of field experts. The course must include field visits in the disaster-prone areas where the students from all over India can go and experience the disasters in reality. The investigators realised that the contribution of each and every person prior, during and after the disaster can create a big beneficial difference, which can help to minimise worst effects of the disaster.

References

Disaster Management in India. (2004) *A Status Report*. Retrieved from https://www.preventionweb.net/files/2534_2534

Disaster Management Act (2005) Retrieved fromhttps://ruralindiaonline.org/en/library/resource

Lawrence, S., and Suresh, (2012). Need for integration of Disaster Management into Engeenering curriculum. *International Journal of Modern Engeenering Research (IJMER),* 2 (6), ISSN:2249-6645. Retrieved fromhttps://citeseerx.ist.psu.edu/viewdoc/download?doi=10.1.1.417.77&rep=rep1&type=pdf

National Disaster Management Plan (2016) *A publication of the National Disaster Management Authority*. Retrieved from https://www.mha.gov.in/sites/default/files/National%20Disaster%20Management%20Plan%20May%202016.pdf

National Policy on Disaster Management (2009) Ministry of Home Affairs. Retrieved fromhttps://nidm.gov.in/PDF/policies/ndm_policy2009.pdf

Shah, A.J. (2011) An overview of disaster management in India. *WIT Transactions on the Built Environment,* 119, ISSN 1743-350. Doi:10.2495/DMAN110081. Retrieved from https://www.witpress.com/Secure/elibrary/papers/DMAN11/DMAN11008FU1.pdf https://ndma.gov.in/Reference_Material/PM_Ten_Agenda

Editors and Contributors

Editors

Dr. M. Rajendra Nath Babu, holds post graduate degrees in Mathematics, Sociology, Psychology, English and M.Ed. (University 1st), M.Phil. and obtained Ph.D. in Education from S.V. University. He got Junior Research Fellow (UGC) award in 2009 and Senior Research Fellow (UGC) award in 2012. He has more than 14 years' research and teaching experience. Presently he is working as Assistant Professor in Department of Teacher Education, Nagaland University (a Central University).

Prof. Santhosh Kumar is a disaster risk reduction, policy planning, and capacity development expert with 25 years of experience in different positions in the development planning and disaster risk reduction sector. With a Ph.D. in Economics, he studied gender and development in the Institute of Development Studies, Sussex, the United Kingdom, and received professional training in disaster risk management from Israel, backed with international work exposure at the World Bank and the Inter-governmental body of South Asian Association for Regional Cooperation. He has an experienced hand in designing, planning, and implementing mitigation and long-term disaster recovery plan and projects.

Prof. Buno Liegise is a Professor and Head, in the Department of Education, Nagaland University. She has over 25 years of teaching experience. She has a foreign-based study experience. She has published more than 30 research works/articles in reputed journals, and edited books. She was formerly Dean of Student‘s Welfare, NU (2003-2006), Head of Department of Education, NU (2009- 2012), Director Incharge Women‘s Studies Centre, NU (2012-2014), Dean, School of Humanities and Education, NU (2014-2017) and also the Administrative and Academic i/c of Kohima Campus, Nagaland University (Sept 2016-July, 2017).

Dr. Kumar Raka is a Social Scientist and a reputed Disaster Management professional. He has earned Masters, M.Phil. and Ph.D. in Sociology from Jawaharlal Nehru University, New Delhi. He has also earned a Masters in Disaster and Emergency Management from Tel Aviv University, Israel. He has more than 12 years of professional experience in Disaster Management. As Planning Specialist & Head of Department, Disaster Management Cell, Noida Authority he established a vibrant Disaster Management mechanism in twin-cities of Noida and Greater Noida and a Mega School Earthquake Evacuation Drill was successfully organized, coordinated & conducted in 110 Schools "on the Same Day at the Same Time" in which about one lakh stakeholders including students and faculties participated. This was the first of its kind mega drill to be conducted by a local authority in the country and earned a place in Limca Book of World Records in 2018 edition.

Dr. Balu I, a Disaster Risk Reduction, Development Management and Capacity Development Professional with 15 years of experience in different positions in the Development Management and Disaster Risk Reduction Sector. A Ph.D in Sociology, studied Development Management from Tata-Dhan Academy, backed with national work exposure at National Institute of Rural Development & Panchayati Raj, Ministry of Home Affairs, Government of India and Rajiv Gandhi National Institute of Youth Development, Ministry of Youth Affairs and Sports, Government of India. Experience of working at the grassroot to national level in all aspects Development Management and Disaster Risk Reduction is an added value. Specialised in Child Centric Disaster Risk Reduction, Youth for Development & Disaster Management. Presently working at National Institute of Disaster Management, Ministry of Home Affairs, Government of India.

Contributors

Dr. Anu G.S., Associate Professor, Department of Education, Nagaland University, Kohima Campus, Meriema, Nagaland-797 004.

Dr. Balu I., CCDRR Centre, National Institute of Disaster Management, Ministry of Home Affairs, Government of India.

C. Hariharan, Assistant Professor, Nehru Memorial College of Education, Puthanampatti, Tiruchirappalli, Tamil Nadu-621 007.

Chhavi Bhalothia, Research Scholar, Toxicology Research Laboratory, Department of Zoology, University College of Science, M.L. Sukhadia University, Udaipur, Rajasthan-313 001.

Dr. Chittibabu Putcha, Assistant Professor, Department of Adult Education, Dr. Harisingh Gour Vishwavidyalaya, Sagar, Madhya Pradesh-470 003.

Deepika Chauhan, Research Scholar, Department of Educational Technology, Bharathidasan University, Tiruchirappalli, Tamil Nadu-620 023.

Eliwon Thiumai, Research Scholar, Department of Education, Indira Gandhi National Tribal University, Amarkantak, Madhya Pradesh-484 887.

Dr. Girima Nagda, Assistant professor, Toxicology Research Laboratory, Department of Zoology, University College of Science, M.L. Sukhadia University, Udaipur, Rajasthan-313 001.

Dr. I. Muthuchamy, Professor & Head, Department of Educational Technology, Bharathidasan University, Tiruchirappalli, Tamil Nadu-620 023.

Dr. M. Mirunalini, Assistant Professor, Department of Educational Technology, Bharathidasan University, Tiruchirappalli, Tamil Nadu-620 024.

Dr. Maria Josephine Arokia Marie. S, Assistant Professor, Department of Education, Indira Gandhi National Tribal University, Amarkantak, Madhya Pradesh-484 887.

Dr. P. Renuka, Associate Professor, Department of Education, Sri Padmavati Mahila Vishvavidhyalayam, Tirupati, Andhra Pradesh-517 502.

Paramesh Roy, Research Scholar, Department of Education, Indira Gandhi National Tribal University, Amarkantak, Madhya Pradesh-484 887.

R. Praveena, Research Scholar, Department of Educational Technology, Bharathidasan University, Tiruchirappalli, Tamil Nadu-620 024.

Rakesh Kumar, Ph.D. Research Scholar, Department of Tribal Studies, Central University of Jharkhand, Ranchi, Jharkhand-835 205.

Rama Verma, Research Scholar, Department of Educational Studies, Central University of Jammu, Jammu and Kashmir-181 143

Dr. Ravi Vanguri, Assistant Professor, Department of Educational Studies, Central University of Jammu, Jammu and Kashmir-181 143.

Dr. Shivdasini Singh Amin, Associate Professor, Department of Humanities and Social Sciences, Mahindra University, Hyderabad, Telangana-500 043.

Dr. V. Mercy Jyothi, Assistant Professor, Department of Education, Dravidian University, Kuppam, Chittoor, Andhra Pradesh-517 426.

Yannam Venkata Mallikarjuna Reddy, Research Scholar, Department of Humanities and Social Sciences, Mahindra University, Hyderabad, Telangana-500 043.